Reviewed by Richard Camp in ~~

American Historical R~

1979), 425-426

by Peter Iver Kaufman in Church History, 49 (September, 1980), 344-345

by John D. Root in the Catholic Historical Review, LXVI (July, 1980), 430-432

CATHOLICISM AND HISTORY

OWEN CHADWICK

CATHOLICISM
AND
HISTORY

THE OPENING OF THE VATICAN ARCHIVES

The Herbert Hensley Henson Lectures
in the University of Oxford, 1976

CAMBRIDGE UNIVERSITY PRESS
CAMBRIDGE
LONDON   NEW YORK   MELBOURNE

Published by the Syndics of the Cambridge University Press
The Pitt Building, Trumpington Street, Cambridge CB2 1RP
Bentley House, 200 Euston Road, London NW1 2DB
32 East 57th Street, New York, NY10022, USA
296 Beaconsfield Parade, Middle Park, Melbourne 3206, Australia

First published 1978

Printed in Great Britain at the
University Press, Cambridge

Library of Congress Cataloguing in Publication Data
Chadwick, Owen.
Catholicism and history.

(The Herbert Hensley Henson lectures in the University
of Oxford ; 1976)

Bibliography: p.

Includes index.

1. Vatican. Archivio vaticano. 2. Papacy – History.
3. Freedom of information in the Church. 4. Catholic
Church – Historiography. 5. Church history – Historiog-
raphy. I. Title. II. Series.
CD1581.C47   282′.09   77-77740
ISBN 0 521 21708 3

Contents

Acknowledgements

My thanks are specially due to Mgr Charles Burns at the Vatican Secret Archives; Mgr Alfons Stickler the prefect, and Mgr J. Ruysschaert the vice-prefect, at the Vatican Library; Father Josef Metzler at the library of the Congregation de Propaganda Fide; Freifrau Auguste von Pastor; the Fathers of the Oratory at Sta Maria Nuova in Vallicella; Father Francis Edwards, S.J., of Farm Street, London; and the trustees of the Hensley Henson Lectureship.

Introduction

By common agreement all governments restrict access to their papers. For a time at least reason of state demands that historians be allowed no access. The British government has brought this time down to thirty years – but only for that majority of papers which reason of state allows. The needs of government and the wishes of the historian conflict.

Acton, who was as personally engaged in the problem as any historian, defined it as *the enmity between the truth of history and the reason of state, between sincere quest and official secrecy.*[1]

Two different kinds of institution generate special difficulty of this nature. One is a personal monarchy. The Queen makes the Royal Archives available to authorized enquirers. But the Royal Archives contain not only some records of government but the papers of a private family, and a family is entitled to that privacy conceded to every other less prominent family. The other special case is a Church, especially the Roman Catholic Church.

Certain key-words made fanatics more fanatical: words like Pope, Jesuit, Index, Inquisition. If you open all the archives until thirty years ago, you open them to historians. You open them also to minds eager to find what discredits. Is it possible that the impartiality of history is better served if the archives are closed than if they are open? Since feelings roused by religions run as deep in the human soul as passions roused by national conflict, the events of the past live in the present. Whether agents of the Church punish a man for saying that the earth went round the sun – whether the Council of Trent was no true ecumenical Council because the Pope controlled marionette bishops on invisible wires – whether a Pope was personally immoral – all these might afford matter for the obsessed, and might even affect attitudes among minds which were not obsessed. They all happen to be questions which only the archives might answer. In this argument between *truth of history* and *reason of state*, reason of state could be found arguing for a much longer closure of archives than that which advanced liberal governments came to adopt.

Modern history, sometimes called loosely 'scientific' history, made such progress during the middle of the last century that its new face affected all men's attitudes towards the past, and therefore some men's attitude towards the present. The principles or beliefs inherited in European tradition came under a new kind of examination. This touched all European culture. How and in what ways it affected culture is an intractable problem of intellectual history; whether it had its impact in ideals of education, or in personal approaches to literature, or in the evolutionary stances adapted from biology into other sciences, or in the analysis of politics and systems of government. To find tests of influences like these is doubtful work. Men's perspective towards life or society changed because they gained a more informed perspective in looking at the past. But how it changed, and how a picture of the world was altered, what difference was made to culture or viewpoint or morals, these aspects of the question are hard to test and not easy even to illustrate.

But religion is a realm where the enquiry sees results. The two akin religions of nineteenth-century Europe, Christianity and Judaism, are in their different ways religions in which history matters. The context of devotion and prayer, though of this moment, is nourished by the memory of past events. The body of doctrine is linked to men and women who lived, and to experiences which they endured, and records bearing the evidence concerning their human destiny. The Jewish and Christian memories were once identified with the historical perspectives of Europe. Religion had more sense of continuity with the past than any other element in the heritage which made up culture among the peoples. The ablest writers among early modern historians were students of Church history.

Therefore the coming of modern history, with its organization of libraries, and publication of manuscripts, and founding of learned journals, and slow creation of endowed posts for historians, could be seen to foster a view of the past which must influence religious attitudes, doctrines, and prayers. This happened in all the Christian Churches.

Among the Churches the Roman Catholic Church faced the challenge in ways which specially interest the historian of ideas. Conservative by inheritance of centuries, more conservative by resistance to radicals in the age of Reformation, ultra-conservative because in many countries a society of peasants or labourers who of all classes had minds least open to disturbing ideas, it was nevertheless a Church committed to history; that is, it could not sweep the challenge behind the door or pretend that it all sprang from infidel illusion. Some of the founders of modern history – Mabillon, Tillemont, Muratori, to mention only three – were dedicated priests. *Tradition* was important to the structure of doctrine which fed men's faith. To Protestant warriors tradition sounded like a way of closing the eyes to history – accept whatever most men believe today and refuse to ask whether they believed it yesterday. Catholic writers gave too much occasion for this charge. But tradition was continuity, and continuity was history. Commitment to tradition was also commitment to history, and a main reason why the study of Christian history was inescapable in Catholic teaching.

Facing this challenge in the realm of doctrine, Catholic thinkers began to analyse that relation between a belief and its definition in language which Newman called *development.* The idea of development had more than one ground, and was variously expressed, and had diverse consequences. But the momentous part of it was the recognition that history makes a difference to the religious understanding of the world.

A Church committed by principle to historical enquiry, and simultaneously committed by its members to conservative attitudes, must experience inward tension. The worst tension was generated by the argument over the relation between history and dogma. A lesser argument developed over the archives. Because we are committed to historical enquiry, is it our duty to allow free access to private archives, even if we are afraid that those who use the archives might change the understanding of the past, or injure the Church of the present?

The Vatican possessed a famous archive which touched the history of Europe over a thousand years, and specially illuminated the past behaviour of Popes and other leaders of the Catholic Church. About access to this archive the argument became warm.

The political mind argued:

We have enemies in the world. Bad things happened in the past. If we open our archives, we let in not only neutrals who want to understand, or friends who have that sympathy which enables men to understand better, but antagonists seeking to stir up dirt. Such hostile enquiry, especially if misused, hurts the institution; and in hurting the institution, hurts the world which the institution serves.

The historical mind argues:

The Church is committed to truth. The opening of archives is a necessary part of the quest for truth in an age of historical enquiry. Truth is an absolute good. No plea of political welfare can override the commitment. The Church wants to know what really happened. For the sake of that quest it must run the risk that fanatics misuse its documents. Misuse is of the moment, truth becomes a possession.

This is the theme: the argument in Catholicism between the ecclesiastical statesman and the historian in need of truth. Each side had its case to advocate. Each side had inarticulate feelings even where its case was hard to argue. And if I think the historian to have the better cause, you will subtract some bias for the circumstance that it is the historian and not the ecclesiastical statesman who must describe what happened.

From the earliest times the Pope, as head of a great administration, needed papers and books. Perhaps the example of
the Roman emperor's civil service in Constantinople still ruled
Rome, and the Pope kept a repository of papers in the Lateran.
But, like other sovereigns of the Middle Ages, he often carried
his papers round on his travels. As with secular perambula-
tions of this sort, it was an easy way to lose letters. He probably
had no systematic arrangement to collect and preserve letters
and copies of letters until the pontificate of Pope Innocent III
(died 1216) who was a lawyer.

The Pope, being bishop of a city, was more stable in one
town than most medieval rulers. Nevertheless, even early in
the fifteenth century, his main collection of papers was stored
not in Rome but at Avignon. Probably the bulk of his registers
moved from Avignon to Rome before 1431.[2]

Then the invention of printing increased the number of
books, and all earlier forms of keeping books were made
obsolete. Simultaneously the learning of the Renaissance
began interest in manuscripts. In 1475, therefore, the Pope
created a 'library' or rather extended the old library, gave a
regular endowment and better buildings, and appointed a
librarian, the humanist Platina, with a staff.

It was already the best stocked library in Italy. No library
was yet large. It had under 4,000 volumes by 1484, but was
important enough in 1527, when the emperor's army sacked
Rome, to attract looters; less however for the value of manuscripts in a market or in scholarship than for seals in the
making of bullets or for parchment as litter for horses.[3] The
soldiery had no idea of the value of what they tore or burnt.
But several accounts describe the mass of original papal documents lying with precious manuscripts in the street. A lot was
recovered later, or appeared elsewhere in Europe – one
important Roman manuscript, perhaps lost during the sack,
is still in the Bodleian Library. One of the registers of Pope
Alexander VI Borgia was returned in two pieces, with many
pages missing, five years later.[4]

From 1548 the status of the library was raised because

henceforth the librarian was always a cardinal. But the cardinal's work sometimes took precedence over the librarian's work. The first Cardinal-librarian, Marcello Cervini, collected books with passion, created new catalogues, and opened the library to scholars at fixed hours. The second of the Cardinal-librarians was a boy of 14 when he was appointed and, though well-educated for his age, was otherwise qualified by being a nephew of Pope Julius III. However, the existence of a cardinal as figure-head of the library helped the real librarians, custodes, to get more of what they wanted; in this case Guglielmo and Girolamo Sirleto, who in succession, from 1554 to 1572, were excellently fitted to extend the range of the library and its manuscripts. The first steps to collect scattered documents began. Marcello Cervini, formerly the Vatican librarian, became Pope, and searched for manuscripts lost during the sack of Rome, and brought some volumes from Avignon.

One cause of this interest was the desire to publish scholarly editions of ancient texts, partly to meet the pleas of Protestants about the primitive Church. The old documents in the Library were far more important than the new. Despite the collections of medieval popes, the current archives were evidently in poor order when Cardinal Borromeo *started* an attempt to collect the papers of the secretariat.[5] Though papers already existed, and were kept, they were scattered here and there in bundles almost as they came to rest. The archives could not be put into order until they were given a home to inhabit. On 15 June 1565 Pope Pius IV ordered the Cardinal-librarian Mula to make an archive – that is, find a room or rooms where the papers should assemble. They transferred more documents from Avignon to Rome. They did not intend to make access easy or even possible, except to the administrators. The times were bitter, and a brief of 1570 made it more difficult to consult, and impossible to copy, the old manuscripts in the library. They intended more efficient business, not scholarship. Pope Pius V (1566–72) brought 158 more volumes from Avignon to Rome, leaving about 500 volumes still at Avignon.[6] The Vatican was still looking for space adequate for storing these papers in any way that would enable them to be consulted at need.

Throughout Europe printed books poured into men's libraries and by 1575 forced heads of institutions to build new libraries to house their growing collections. In these years the colleges of Cambridge University built their first libraries – one may still be seen almost unchanged, in the old library at Trinity Hall. Between 1587 and 1591, just when the old library at Trinity Hall was under construction, Sixtus V built the Vatican Library as it was to survive until near the end of the nineteenth century; Fontana's magnificent edifice. At first the change was no improvement to those who wished to consult books or papers. It took twenty years before everything was in order after the move; and even then large numbers of books were still uncatalogued. The needs of the library outgrew the endeavours of its exiguous staff, who were paid irregularly, and largely in kind.

The library was open for two or three hours in the day for scholars to consult, though it was shut on frequent holidays. In 1591 Pope Gregory XIV issued a stern order against using documents without his permission.[7] But visitors gained access easily enough. In 1581 Montaigne saw what he liked without difficulty. In 1600[8] Schott talked of the crowds of scholars working in the library, apparently with complete freedom, and only lamented the lack of a proper catalogue. It was a good time, with a dedicated librarian, Domenico Ranaldi, working at arrangement and access, both in the library and the archives. Privileged scholars borrowed books comfortably. Cardinal Caesar Baronius took away a precious Greek manuscript for two months.[9] But these freedoms varied according to the administration, and the excellent works of scholarship which appeared were mostly due to officers of the library or the Curia. In 1652 Heinsius did not arrange to stay long in Rome because (he thought) they would hardly show manuscripts to foreigners.[10]

The archives were seldom accessible in this way. Only privileged members of the Curia consulted them, usually for business, but on rare occasions for history. Odorico Rinaldi used the archives to continue the Annals of Baronius, Pallavicino to write the official history of the Council of Trent.

Slowly library and archive were seen to be incompatible. The library became a treasure-house of ancient manuscripts and rare books, and clamoured to be used. The archive was full of the secret papers of government which unscrupulous men could misuse if they got copies; and the stringent precautions against consulting the archive spilled over into the attitudes to harmless scholars who needed the library. At the end of the sixteenth century Pope Clement VIII started to move archives away from the library and into the Castel Sant' Angelo. This was intended for security. But the papers were not stored in dungeons. They were needed. Busy men wished to find documents quickly. An ornamented hall on the upper floor of the castle was reserved and decorated and furnished with presses.[11] A bull of 1593 was prepared to transfer all the archives to this repository. But second thoughts came, and the bull was never published. It was more convenient to have many of the papers in the Vatican, and the castle was considered a place of special safety for documents of exceptional value or secrecy.

The logical end was division between library and archives. In 1612, therefore, Pope Paul V reversed the policy of moving archives to the castle, but simultaneously separated library from archive as institutions. They were given separate heads. The archives were placed in a long wing of the Vatican Palace by the library. Into this building passed various groups of archives, with a nucleus in the volumes of papal registers which were hitherto kept for ready consultation in the 'wardrobe' above the Pope's apartments. Some of the papers from Sant' Angelo were carried back. But the most valuable or secret documents were still left in the castle for security.

The creation of the Archive – not called officially the Vatican Secret Archives until later – was a sensible act of administration. For until that moment papers lay about in each office. Different bureaux of the civil service still kept what they used. Therefore the new Papal Archive was composed of the specially important papers in Castel Sant' Angelo (like the documents of the Council of Trent), the archive which already existed in the Vatican Library, of which the nucleus was 279 parchment registers from John VIII to Sixtus IV, the very incomplete records of the Secretary of State hitherto in the Castel Sant' Angelo,[12] and the archives of the different offices (especially of the Treasury) which were now put, still with many exceptions, under the control of the central archive. Pope Paul V holds the honour of first creating an independent central archive which began to act like a magnet, slowly drawing towards itself the mass of various collections from various offices.

The creation of a central archive owed nothing to the notion of helping scholars to write history. It was a business transaction intended to make the administration more efficient. The Pope's major-domo was blunt in his material view of the gain. 'Old documents', he said, 'are non-military weapons for holding on to property we have acquired.'[13]

At the archives the officials could not always find the weapon that they wanted. The central collection came from various sources, sometimes piecemeal, some of them already well-arranged, others in disorder, some a complete series and others part of a collection of which the rest lay in the castle or even at Avignon. The miscellany of origin controlled arrangement inside the Archive. Occasionally papers of exceptional importance could not be found. During the weary meetings leading to the Peace of Westphalia which ended the Thirty Years War in 1648, the papal envoy Chigi wished to concoct a protest against unfavourable terms. To this end he needed copies of the papal protest against the terms of the Peace of Augsburg nearly a century before. He applied to Rome. The archivists could find no copy.[14]

That no copy could be found might be due to ill-arrangement or negligence. The various rooms housed a lot of paper, organized by a scholarly but tiny and ill-paid staff. Since, however, they needed to serve no public enquiries, but solely the needs of the administration, they kept pace with the conflux of papers surprisingly. Occasionally they were capable of putting their records to dramatic use.

In the Sala Regia at the Vatican was a picture of the Emperor Frederick Barbarossa and Pope Alexander III, to which was affixed (by Pope Pius IV) an inscription praising the Venetians for rescuing the Pope from the Emperor and restoring him to power. This inscription came to be regarded as humbling to popes. The prefect of the archives proved that the supposed scene never happened, and the inscription (1635) was removed. The government of Venice was offended, and with threats demanded that the inscription be restored. It was not then the Pope's policy to offend Venice, and he was therefore humiliated three times over: first by restoring an inscription thought to be demeaning, second by doing it though he knew it to be untrue, and third by being forced on Venetian demand to relieve of his duties the prefect of the archives.[15]

The chief reason why the archives might be incomplete or copies might not be found, without any negligence of archivists, lay in the family nature of papal government. Nominally until 1692, but actually until later, popes used their nephews in the administration. A bulk of papers came to the Pope's nephew as representative of the Pope and so, when the Pope died and the nephew held office no longer, became part of the family papers. In this way important sections of the Pope's administrative records came to rest, not in the Vatican Archives, but in the libraries or cupboards of great Roman families like the Borghese, Barberini, Chigi, Pamfili, Farnese, Caetani, Albani. The papers of the last non-Italian Pope, Adrian VI, were lost altogether because at his death his secretary carried them away to Liège and they were never afterwards found.[16] The documents of Pope Marcellus II concerning the Council of Trent, collected in fifty-four volumes, remained in his Cervini family until just before the French Revolution, when they passed into the archive of the library at Florence.[17] Some of the Borghese papers still lie in the John Rylands Library at Manchester, whither they passed from the collection of the Earl of Crawford and Balcarres. Most of the others remained in the family until 1891 when they were bought by Pope Leo XIII.

The archives remained shut. But they did not remain unaltered. In the course of the seventeenth century the new office of Secretary of State grew towards its modern importance. Little by little the government of the Curia ceased to be a family business and became more like a civil service. Therefore the head of that civil service, the Secretary of State, steadily became more important, especially as the drafter of letters to the nuncios in various capitals and the recipient of reports from the nuncios. It was a mark of the development of the office of Secretary of State when in 1656 the Pope ordered that his records be no longer left in the care of individual secretaries but be transferred to the archives. The archives had received some records of the Secretary of State from Castel Sant' Angelo in 1614, and in 1630 the important reports of nuncios from the sixteenth century.[18] But the decision of 1656 was a landmark in the history of the archives, for henceforth the bulk of accessions came from the office of the Secretary of State.

The archive was a different institution from the library – in name, constitution, and partly in reality. Since Paul V separated them, they went their different ways – for the library was art and the archives business. The library was headed by a cardinal, the archives only by a custos or prefect. During the eighteenth century the officers in the archives began to feel the need of some resource to whom they could turn for help, especially in the struggle for funds. They did not turn to the Cardinal-librarian, but to the Secretary of State, who now controlled the allocation of funds in the Vatican. This constitutional relation between the Cardinal-Secretary of State and the archives helped to draw the two institutions of library and archives further apart; except in the rare periods when the Secretary of State also took for himself the office of Cardinal-librarian.

The aims of the institutions were different. No one was

allowed in the archive, except Pope and Secretary of State for purpose of business, or someone under their immediate orders. If the library grew more difficult of access, the archives were never in theory open to anyone outside the administration. But the atmosphere of one affected the other. The archive was a junior institution, without a cardinal at its head. In the free-and-easy age of the library, the staff of the archives were inclined to behave in a free-and-easy way; so that in 1737 Cardinal Acquaviva, who acted wholly in the interests of the King of Spain, got to see the vital letters of the Secretary of State, even those that were in cipher, on payment of a suitable fee to the staff.[19] When the library was shut close, the archive was shut closer.

Both institutions were part of the Pope's 'family' – that is, archivists, like the staff of the library, were treated to allowances of bread and commons and received pay as members of the household. Though the institutions were already of international importance, they were both the Pope's private institutions, his collection of books and manuscripts for study or for art, and his cabinet for filing letters.

The staff of the archive was too small for the flow of papers. At the beginning of his reign (1740) the scholarly Pope Benedict XIV was told by the archivist that they sometimes found it hard to find diplomatic documents which the Secretary of State wanted. Benedict XIV improved the pay and provided assistants to help with the catalogue and encouraged Giuseppe Garampi to establish order. The task was so large and impossible, Garampi once told the Pope, that it was small wonder if the archivists shrank from attempting a work which they could never finish. 'To make a catalogue needs a hundred men all working hard.'[20] The lists which Garampi made were useful into the twentieth century.

In the seventies of the eighteenth century not all was well-ordered. When the Pope needed the copy of a brief by which a predecessor suppressed the monastery of Port-Royal, he had to beg the favour of a copy from the French ambassador. Four years later the King of Saxony astonished Rome by mentioning a vicar-apostolic of Saxony, that is, the Pope's special representative as substitute for the bishop. The Curia had never heard of a vicar-apostolic of Saxony. The archivists hunted for traces of the office and found none. They must have looked either shamefaced or sceptical when the Saxon envoy produced a solemnly authenticated copy of the relevant brief.[21]

In 1783 the last volumes still held at Avignon were moved to Rome.

Then came the French Revolution, the French armies in Italy, and French generals in Rome. Suddenly the academic world became interested in these archives, the more interested because they were inaccessible.

2

The record of Galileo's trial:
Marino Marini

The Emperor Napoleon Bonaparte had a vision of a lasting empire in Europe ruled by the French. As part of his dream, he would organize the history and art of Europe, collecting the loveliest paintings into the Louvre, the fairest manuscripts into the Bibliothèque Nationale, and the archives of European capitals into a central archive to be built in Rheims or (later) Paris. He found the dream practicable, and sent orders to his governors. On 18 December 1809 the French officer in Rome, General Miollis, received the command to send the whole archive of the Pope to France. Only a few months before, the French government kidnapped the Pope.

By various convoys, beginning in February 1810 and ending in February 1811 (with a last convoy in 1813), wagon-trains filled with chests of documents passed along the roads to Turin, and over the Mont-Cenis pass to Paris. Eight chests fell into a ditch near Susa, and two carts were carried away by a flood at Borgo San Donnino.[1] The operation cost the French government more than 600,000 francs. In June 1810 the French chief archivist, ex-Oratorian Daunou, who was an anticlerical and disapproved of popes, asked the Pope's archivist, Gaetano Marini, why some documents were missing. Gaetano Marini, who had already much experience trying to protect his archives from the revolutionary government in Rome, had to confess that he hid them in Rome before leaving; and thus the *Liber Diurnus*, then believed to be the ancient formulary which admitted popes to their office, the golden bulls which were bulls with the seal stamped upon gold for specially solemn acts, of which the Vatican Archives possessed a priceless collection of 78 ranging from the Holy Roman Emperor Frederick Barbarossa in 1164 to the Italian republic a few years before,[2] and the acts of the Council of Trent which had always been regarded as specially secret and of unique importance, also crossed the Alps. A total of 3,239 chests reached Paris, only a few less than left Rome. The French counted what arrived. They calculated it at 102,435 registers, volumes or bundles. They omitted to ask for the records of the reigning Pope, which were buried in the gardens of the Vatican and not recovered for nearly fifty years.[3]

This enormous bulk of paper was brought to the Palais Soubise, until the Emperor had time to build a Record Office for all Europe. In the Palais Soubise Daunou started to put the documents into new order, by making catalogues and rearranging. The rearrangement might have been excellent if it had been complete. As Daunou lost control of the archive before he finished, rearrangement was synonym for introducing confusion. The archives lost something of the piecemeal system of their old organization, without acquiring a new organization. This was not Daunou's fault. Though he was anticlerical, he was an honourable man who did all in his power to keep the archives safe and put them into order. The one danger lay in Daunou's willingness to allow scholars to use the unique opportunity to gain access to hitherto inaccessible papers, and even to allow borrowers of high rank and presumed integrity, a presumption not always warranted. But the archives suffered little loss in Paris. The damage hit them when they returned.

For Napoleon at last was beaten, and on 31 March 1814 the allied armies entered Paris. Only three weeks later the new authorities ordered that the archives be restored to Rome. In May 1814 a first load of important matter, including ceremonial necessities, the ornaments of the Pope's private chapel, a mitre given by the Queen of Etruria, a tiara given by Napoleon at his coronation, were sent off to Rome. But the archives cost 600,000 francs to bring to Paris, and no one had anything like that sum to take them back; and while the papal archivist Marino Marini (Gaetano's nephew) packed chests and wondered how much he could do for the 60,000 francs which was all the new French government would or could provide, Napoleon left Elba and landed in France; and in the hectic weeks before the battle of Waterloo, his servants found time to cancel the restoration of the archives and again put Daunou in charge. Marino Marini, whose famous and learned uncle Gaetano died in Paris that March, went home to Italy. After the final fall of Napoleon, Marino Marini returned to Paris and at the end of October sent off the first load of chests by land to Rome. The chests contained what Rome most urgently wanted: part of the privy archives, the archives of Propaganda, of the Secretariat of Briefs, part of the archive of the Inquisition, and of the Congregation of the Council.[4] Marino Marini heard that they were in danger because the escort of soldiers caused unrest among the people as they passed. He hurried after them, and caught them just as one of the chests was damaged by falling in the River Taro. He accompanied them all the way to Rome.

And still the cost of transport was prohibitive. Daunou suggested that they could safely reduce the bulk by destroying one-third of the papers which lay along the corridors of the Palais Soubise, arguing that such papers were of no interest to politicians, historians or churchmen. Marino Marini, who started by opposing the idea, slowly came round. He now extended the proposal; not only to burn the archive of 'the Bishops and Regulars' and part of the Penitentiary and Rota, but to burn all the archives of the Inquisition; with the probable intention not of removing useless paper, but of removing paper that one day might hurt the Church. In June 1816 Cardinal Consalvi circulated the departments of the administration in Rome asking whether they had papers in Paris which they regarded as 'useless', and so could reduce the costs of return. Nearly all the departments wanted to get back all their papers. Propaganda replied that the useless papers had already arrived and they needed the others. One congregation gave warning that packages labelled useless should not be so treated because the labels were affixed to important bundles with the aim of deceiving the French.[5] Four minor congregations, including that for the fabric of St Peter's and that for the Pontine marshes, reported that they had lost no papers.

But the new papal agent in Paris, Count Ginnasi, was already selling paper by weight. Late in 1817 the first wagon-train (174 chests) came to Rome by sea from Marseilles, to avoid the greater expenses of the route by land. A second train (200 chests), a third (153) and a fourth (42) followed by land. They did not arrive without damage, especially from water in crossing streams, and by loss of some volumes. Cardinal Consalvi was not content. That summer he sent back Monsignor Marino Marini to tidy what was becoming a mess.

In July 1817 999 chests went off by sea, the majority by the brig *Neptune* from Le Havre; 259 more chests went off by land. Seventeen of the chests, which were stored at the bottom of the hold of the *Neptune*, were found to be damaged by water when they arrived at Civita Vecchia.[6] The last wagon-train by land did not arrive in Rome till mid-December 1817.

The archives went to Paris in 3,239 chests. They came back in about 2,200 chests. If we assume that the chests were roughly equal, about one-third of the archives that went to Paris never came back.

They went under public escort, at a cost to the European tax-payer, of over 600,000 French francs. They returned, under private contract, not always well-organized, in trouble at customs-ports, for a cost to the French tax-payer of one-tenth of that sum, some tens of thousands of francs more from the Pope's coffers – though in the interval the cost of transport rose. The losses of archives were caused not by their kidnapping but by their return.

While Ginnasi was in charge, he sold a lot of archives by weight to a grocer. What they were is not precisely known. They were bulky enough, for he received 15,000 French francs. They certainly included some Inquisition trial records, and registers of the Datary. (The Datary supervised the conferment of ecclesiastical posts and hence was in part a taxing and in part a dispensing authority. Therefore it was bitterly criticized in the age of the Renaissance and early Reformation as an organ of the hunt for money. Since 1588 it had authority in marriage dispensations. Its registers were commonly known as the Lateran registers because they were kept at the Lateran Palace.)

The cardinal in charge of the Datary, known till the twentieth century as the Prodatary, was vexed at this behaviour of Count Ginnasi and at the losses in his records. When Marino Marini came back to Paris he bought back 2,400 volumes of these Lateran registers but did not seek to recover the Inquisition records. On the contrary he sold 2,600 more volumes of Inquisition records to a manufacturer of cardboard, first shredding the papers and putting them in water to make them illegible. From these sales he helped to pay his expenses. He preferred Parisians not to know that he tore up Inquisition records lest the destruction gave rise to unseemly jests.[7] (Two years later he bought back thirty-seven volumes of Inquisition records, evidently some of those which Count Ginnasi sold unshredded.)

Despite the reproaches of the Prodatary against Ginnasi, Marini also sold some Datary records, and some papers of the Consulta which was one of the two committees for the government of the papal states. These sales by Marini gained only 5,500 francs, and therefore may have been less numerous than the sales by Count Ginnasi. But probably this was not so, for after shredding and immersion, the documents were less interesting.

Fragments of former papal archives could occasionally be bought in Paris shops till late in the nineteenth century.

Thirteen volumes from the Lateran registers are now in the library of Trinity College, Dublin.

The Bibliothèque Nationale in Paris sooner or later acquired groups of miscellaneous material especially concerning the canonization of saints, an Inquisition register, a register from another congregation.

Meanwhile the imperial archivist Daunou trusted too many borrowers, or suffered the loss of responsibility before they returned what they removed. Thieves abstracted certain important papers. The letters of Bossuet and of other French bishops naturally interested French Gallican bishops. Marini found that the originals of the trials before the suppression of the Templars had vanished; and the records of the trial of Galileo; the volume containing the brief which turned Bishop Talleyrand back into a layman; some volumes of the papal registers, especially of Pope Julius II.[8] Marini went round trying to recover these papers, with very partial success. He sought earnestly for the Galileo papers, and failed. He was filled with indignation at the way in which French officials treated him over these thefts. But the French government fell three times within a year, so that disorder in the administration could not surprise.

The removal of the archives to Paris and their return swung the attention of the learned world to the historical importance of the archives. No one had known what they contained. During the short time that the French looked after them, the keepers started to index. The French archivists made lists, partly because they were good archivists, and partly because their head Daunou was an anticlerical looking for propaganda against popes. These indexes were neither adequate nor complete. But they were indexes, the first rough guide available to anyone except two or three men at Rome. The scholars who saw what Daunou could find published their little harvest, bit by bit, to the world. By 1820 learned Europe was more conscious of a treasure of historical documents locked away in Rome.

Marino Marini slowly rearranged the papers and got them back into better order. But the consequences of the French misappropriation were not remedied for decades. The archives hardly recovered until 1883 or 1890 the order which they possessed before the French confiscated.

The Galileo papers vanished in Paris. Marino Marini the Pope's archivist hunted everywhere, and was able to discover a lot about them, but the trail kept failing. With all the rest of the archives of the Inquisition they went to Paris in 1810. The French archivist Daunou gave instructions (3 January 1811) that his team were to look in the Vatican Archives for documents which showed how popes abused their spiritual powers against the authority of kings and the peace of peoples.[9] The French imperial agents were impartial cataloguers, but wanted to uncover information which might help to discredit popes. Naturally the papers of the Inquisition were an obvious treasure; and of all the trials of the Inquisition the most discreditable in repute was the condemnation of Galileo for asserting (as was said) that the earth goes round the sun. The French looked for, and at once found, the Galileo papers.

Napoleon heard, was interested, asked to see the documents. The state librarian, Alexander Barbier, made a copy. Barbier suggested that the originals, Latin and Italian, be published with a French translation. Napoleon agreed, and gave him the task.

Then Napoleon fell, and the allied armies entered Rome, and Marini hurried round the ministries looking for Galileo's papers. On the point of receiving them, he heard that the restored King of France wanted to read them, and that he should have them back as soon as the king had finished. But before the king finished, Napoleon landed from Elba, and the king fled, and the Galileo papers again disappeared. Marino Marini, still on the scent, chasing them from ministry to ministry, came at last upon the assurance that they were burnt when the king fled.

Marini was disturbed when in 1820 an Italian editor, Venturi, published at Modena part of the trial records. Venturi applied to Paris; and though Paris could not find the originals, they had the extracts which Barbier made, and a large fragment of a French translation.[10] These were the basis of Venturi's edition. It renewed the pressure upon Paris from Rome, and renewed public interest in records of the Inquisition that might be hidden in Rome.

In 1828 another search in Paris failed to find the missing

documents. Rome applied again seven years later, and still another search failed. Eleven years after that it was suddenly discovered that they were back in Rome.

Where had they been, and how had they returned? Afterwards everyone believed the following story: that the French ambassador in Rome, Pellegrino Rossi, made efforts to get them from the French government; that they were found in the archives of the French Foreign Ministry; and that King Louis Philippe restored them to the Pope on condition that they were published. This story was widely believed at the time, and never contradicted. Not until 1926 was the truth discovered.[11] One of the French ministers, to whom Marino Marini applied unsuccessfully, was the Comte de Blacas. Blacas denied to Marini that he had the papers or knew where they were kept. In fact he had them all the time. At the revolution of 1830 Blacas followed the King into his exile at Prague. When he died in Vienna, his widow found the Galileo records among his papers. In 1843 she gave them to the nuncio in Vienna to give to the Pope.

Still, by whatever route the Galileo papers returned to Rome, it was known that they were back in Rome. Instantly the pressure began.

Not to have the documents was pleasant (provided, that is, that no one else had got them). Men more freely expect to publish documents when they have no responsibility for deciding whether to publish. The commissary of the Inquisition in Rome was asked for the documents in 1830 and said that they did not have them – 'had we possessed them, there would have been no difficulty in communicating them to you'.[12] While the documents were away, it was easy to say that they could be published. Once the documents were back, differences arose.

The differences were sharpened because with the Pope's approval the archivist Marino Marini began to release documents from the archives. International scholars began to knock at the archivist's door, and made applications which he could not resist with too churlish a rigidity.

The first half of the nineteenth century saw the age of historical revival. History as subject or science came into its kingdom. Therefore historians began to press upon the doors of every important archive, from Simancas to St Petersburg. The British government, which neglected its official papers and allowed many of them to rot in a damp store, was soon forced into that course of improvement which created the Public Record Office. Berlin was the first to provide a service which satisfied scholars. Other capitals moved more slowly. If Rome moved slowly it was not exceptional. But Rome had special reasons, or fancied that it had special reasons, for discouraging enquiry.

In that same generation *nationality* became a key-word in politics. If Germany or Italy hitherto were only a political idea, and were now becoming 'nations', everyone wanted to know the meaning of *nation*, and this was best observed by students of language and of history. Every civilized country was suddenly more interested in its 'national origins'. This quest for national history made the Vatican Archives more important. The roots of modern nations were planted in the Middle Ages. Documents from that age, though plentiful in London or Paris, were less plentiful in Prague or Edinburgh or Turin. As an international supreme court of the Middle Ages, the Vatican received continual applications or appeals from all over Europe. Historians believed that, if allowed access in Rome, they might gain much light upon the history of their nation.

The Germans were first in the field. On Christmas Eve 1821 G. H. Pertz, founding editor of that noble collection which was to serve the national history of Germany, the *Monumenta Germaniae Historica*, entered Rome. He went to the Prussian ambassador, the historian Niebuhr, and said that he needed access to the Vatican Archives. Niebuhr discouraged. He 'thought, from what he knew of the Italians, and judging by the experience of other scholars, that I should never be able to gain access to the Vatican Archives, and that it would be very difficult to obtain admission to the Vatican Library'.[13] Nine months later Pertz, to his own surprise, found that his

22

friends had won him leave to copy documents from the archives. He might not go in, for under the rule anyone (but the staff) who went in was excommunicated. Marino Marini could not take him to the shelves. But he invited him to his apartment in the Palazzo Cesi and there brought him documents for study; which a secretary might copy as Marino Marini directed, and then each extract must be seen and certified by the archivist. Naturally Pertz must pay a fee for each document.

So in the morning Pertz worked for three hours at the library, and in the afternoon for three hours at Marini's apartment; starting to copy the documents in the registers of Pope Honorius III which touched German history. He copied or excerpted 1,800 documents out of about 24,000 which he perused. Later he made a famous sentence, destined to quotation: 'There is no better defence of the Papacy than to unveil its inward being. If weakness is shown up, you can reckon on a more friendly judgment through historical understanding than if, as often until now, it is all kept secret and men are left to suspect what they will.'[14]

This was an important moment in the history of history. For the first time a stranger gained access, not to the archives which would have made him excommunicate, but to documents from the Vatican Secret Archives, though he was a Protestant and though he was young and untried, solely for the interests of scholarship, and because the Secretary of State Cardinal Consalvi respected the Prussians. November 1822 may be set by July 1879 as a date in the history of the discovery of truth in history.

Other nations followed the Prussian example. The Roman Curia discovered advantage in what was happening. Since the Counter-Reformation the city of Rome was no longer a key to the politics of Europe. In compensation the popes of the eighteenth century made the city the centre of European art and archaeology. Now the Curia realized that it was also a centre of European scholarship in an age when scholarship became powerful.

The Vatican Library was an institution distinct from the Vatican Archives. But the two institutions were housed in the same block of buildings, and outsiders were not always aware that they were different. Through all the nineteenth century some applicants turned to the Vatican Library when what they needed was the Archives, and vice versa. They were under different management and went their separate ways. But because they lived side by side, and because many non-Romans imagined them to be two departments of one institution, the reputation of the library affected the reputation of the archives. As the manuscripts of the library became more accessible, men fancied that *therefore* the documents in the archive were more accessible.

For in this same age, the second quarter of the nineteenth century, the Vatican Library first gained its true importance in international scholarship. Its prefect from 1819 to 1853 was Angelo Mai, the renovator of classical studies. To the enthusiasm of the world he found in the Vatican Library fragments of Cicero's book *De republica*. His monumental editions of classical authors and of the Fathers appeared year by year. The techniques were controversial, the editorial methods extraordinary, the person generated argument and sometimes passion. But Angelo Mai opened to an excited Europe a glimpse of the historical treasure contained in the Vatican.

Cardinals who continued to think it easy to keep inquisitive eyes away from the Pope's private papers had no idea how many hands would soon be knocking at their doors. They were like keepers of a museum who tantalized an eager public by keeping the museum shut and occasionally showing select objects through the bars of a narrow window. But to show objects brought advantage. If Angelo Mai could make the library a focus of European scholarship, Marino Marini might make the archives a focus of European history. He might also supplement an exiguous stipend with fees.

As Pertz worked away at his German archives in Marino Marini's apartment in the Palazzo Cesi, Marini suddenly said

to Pertz that he was considering for which European nation
he would copy archives. 'He thought England, being the
richest country, would pay him best.'[15] Marino Marini's vision
of work for English history was fulfilled. An agent of the
British government appeared in Rome two years later, and
made an agreement whereby Marino Marini supplied for
appropriate fees copies of those documents in the Vatican
Secret Archives which concerned British history. Fifty volumes
of copies came to the Master of the Rolls, until the Home
Secretary ordered that they be transferred to the British
Museum, where they may still be read as Additional Manuscripts 15,351–15,400. A note at the beginning of the first of
these volumes records the agreement with Marino Marini.[16]

Other governments did likewise: France, Sardinia, Prague,
Vienna, Russia. Marino Marini organized the copying.

It was tantalizing. No one might enter the archives under
pain of excommunication. No one could see adequate catalogues because no adequate catalogues existed. No one could
check whether the copy provided by Marino Marini was
faithful to its original. No one could discover whether they
received a full set, or a fair selection, or even a bowdlerized
selection. No one but official representatives of a government
could gain even this permission. Scholars working for their
governments were not confident either of the completeness
or of the accuracy of Marino Marini's handiwork. Pertz
observed that Marino Marini's effective staff consisted of one
secretary with a tiny stipend, who could hardly decipher the
simplest abbreviations in medieval manuscripts.[17] Pertz's
colleague Johann Friedrich Böhmer, was pleased with the
freedom which Marino Marini allowed. Even so, delay after
delay; he had to wait till the volumes, one by one, were
brought to Marino Marini's apartment, where he could only
work for a little more than two hours a day, and this time was
reduced by gossipy conversation. 'I feel personally hurt that
it is all so dreary. What a benefit to the Church as well as to
scholarship if it were otherwise.' Böhmer went away and
drafted a ferocious attack upon the policy pursued by the

managers of the Vatican Library and Archives; in his cruellest passage accusing the staff of wanting no improvement because any improvement would make them less indispensable. He mellowed, and never published this attack, which was found among his papers after his death. But one of Böhmer's sentences, from a private letter, was destined to be quoted again and again, until it became canonized as a motto:

Please God that the next Pope, whom prophets have hoped for as a light from heaven, will look upon a truth-loving study of history as a light coming down from God to shine in our darkness and show us how we go astray in this modern age![18]

No government could have a national interest in the publication of the record of Galileo's trial. The pressure upon the Curia was not the wish of a legitimate pride in a nation's history. To the Curia it looked like – and sometimes it was – the inquisitiveness of fanatics. They saw no reason why they should publish, and good reason why they should not.

The condemnation of Galileo was not a creditable performance. If the documents were published, they drew attention again – if not again and again – to the discreditable nature of what happened.

To the contrary: though the condemnation was discreditable, it was less discreditable than rumours about the trial. Historians widely believed, and widely stated in print, that Galileo was seized by Inquisitors; maintained his opinion; was tortured, and in agony yielded; knelt, clad only in his shirt, before a court of the Inquisition and solemnly recanted; rose indignant, stamped his foot, and said *All the same, it does move*; was thrown into a dungeon and (in some accounts) had his eyes put out; and spent long months in prison, the story varying from seven years to one year. (The true length of his imprisonment was one day over three weeks.)

When reality was bad, truth was almost always less bad than rumours which sprang up if truth was uncertain, and especially if the guardians of the documents were suspected of hiding what they did not dare to allow into the light.

The Curia was slow to accept this last argument. And the cardinals were slow to realize – for most of the century they hardly realized – how the selective and advantageous release of archives for the benefit of government made refusal to release archives (unless contemporary or near-contemporary) look more and more like a conscious effort to hide. They had an excellent reason for not admitting the world into the archives – namely that the papers were not in excellent order before the French Revolution; that the French left them in worse disorder; that they had neither money nor staff either to put them into order or to cope with a flood of enquiries. But this was an argument uncomfortable to use; and could not justify a refusal of the Galileo papers, which were not lost because they were known to be just returned after being stolen by the French.

The Galileo papers did not belong to the Vatican Archives. They formed part of the archives of the Inquisition, which had never been, and still are not (however desirable that they should be) transferred to the care of the Vatican Archives. When they came back to Rome in the eighteen-forties, no one had decided where they should go, nor how to accede to a French desire that they be published. And while this question was under debate, came the Roman revolution of 1848, and in November of that year the Pope fled to Gaeta, and soon all his institutions and property fell under the control of revolutionary and republican government.

The Holy Office of the Inquisition was not only a historical survival. It was still part of the administration of law and police in Rome and the papal states, and as such was unpopular. Its buildings were a natural target for a mob. Soon after the Pope fled from Rome, the government – a government weakening daily – put civil guards at the buildings of the Inquisition to prevent them being looted.

Silvestro Gherardi arrived in Rome towards the end of 1848 and occupied station among the revolutionary leaders; first a member of the constituent assembly to decide upon a republican constitution, then Secretary of State, finally minister of education in the republican government. Soon after the flight of Pope Pius IX from Rome, he searched the archives of the Inquisition, not in any sense as a looter but while guards protected the offices. He looked for but could not find the Galileo documents. He discovered the archives in some disorder, seeming as though the custodians, when they fled from the republicans, snatched up papers as they ran.[19]

Gherardi found that the archives of the Inquisition were arranged in three divisions: (1) the sittings and decisions of the congregation, bound together in a series under the title of *Decreta*, (2) the examinations of witnesses, acts of trials and sentences, bound together in a series under the title of *Processus*, (3) an index called *Rubricelle*. The series of *Processus* appeared to have many gaps. Gherardi turned to the *Decreta*, and (much helped by a learned friend whom afterwards he refused to name) started to find separate documents on Galileo. Then by good fortune he came across a bundle of thirty-two documents about the Galileo case. This collection he took.

In April 1849 the French were at the gates, and the city became insecure. After the republican government secularized all the property of the Church it made an order that the buildings of the Inquisition be converted into tenements for the poor.[20] Even if the archives had been safe, which they were not, they must be moved. With certain other libraries they were therefore moved into the church of St Apollinare. Here Gherardi had time to take another look at them, but briefly. On 4 July 1849 the French General Oudinot marched into Rome to restore the Pope to his lawful authority. Gherardi had one more quick look at his papers after the French marched in, and then fled. He sought refuge in Genoa.

But he did not yet publish the documents. The reason became plain twenty years later. In his flight he had not removed most of the documents. Though he took ten of them with him he left the others somewhere in Rome. Only twenty years later could he return safely to Rome, and publish what he found during the anarchy.[21]

Meanwhile in Rome, the whereabouts of the main papers in the Galileo case were disclosed. During the revolution the Pope gave them for safe-keeping to Monsignor Marino Marini. Whether Marini lodged them in a cupboard in the Vatican is not known. But the diligence of Silvestro Gherardi could not find them.

In March 1850 Pope Pius IX returned from his exile. He was in very conservative mood. He had a new Secretary of State, Cardinal Antonelli, who was also very conservative and was not interested in scholarship.

On 8 May 1850 he visited the Vatican Archives. Into the hands of Monsignor Marino Marini he gave the missing Galileo papers. Thus these papers,[22] formerly part of the archives of the Inquisition, became part of the Vatican Secret Archives proper.

It was understood that the French wanted them published. Marini was now charged with such a publication. He worked rapidly, and printed that same autumn a slim volume, entitled *Galileo e l'Inquisizione*. It summarized, or quoted from, a number of previously unknown documents. Thus it was the first attempt to publish from the originals. With Venturi's use of the French copies in 1820, and Marini's little book, it was beginning to be possible to document the famous trial.

But Marini's book caused discontent. Men believed that the documents were returned by the French on condition that they were published. No one could say that this condition was met by Marini's book. Cries of bad faith were heard, of 'dread of public opinion', 'hatred of truth'.[23] Moreover, Marini's book contained more than documents. The tone was defensive. It preferred the behaviour of the Inquisition to the behaviour of Galileo.[24] Gherardi called it an insolent, clumsy little book. Certainly it represented the Inquisitors as morally indefensible if they failed to condemn Galileo.

With this little book Marino Marini believed that he had done all that history needed. The aftermath of revolution was not favourable to liberal policy. Even the privileges formerly accorded to the envoys of governments were now insecure. When the Belgian government sent a scholar in 1853 to investigate the records of early Belgian history Cardinal Antonelli replied to the Belgian minister to the Holy See, 'Entry to the archives is forbidden to everyone under pain of excommunication.'[25]

Marino Marini was growing old, and suffering in health. His time was passing, and the responsibility bit by bit transferred to an archivist different in outlook and temper.

3

The Record of Galileo's Trial:
Theiner

For nearly half a century Monsignor Marino Marini cared for
the Vatican Archives. His important service was the rescue of
papers in Paris at the fall of Napoleon. Then he directed the
archives with sense and friendliness to scholarly enquiries.
Despite a derisory staff to help him he provided copies of
documents which touched the history of various countries, and
several famous scholars worked at papers in his private
apartment. He could read medieval script easily enough, but
otherwise was better equipped to be a copyist than a critical
student of the documents he controlled. And his editions
were somehow suspected of incompleteness not caused by
inadvertent omission. The director of the archives of the
French foreign ministry reported a case where two different
sets of copies of Vatican originals existed, one set by Chateaubriand and the other set by Marini; and in Marini he found
'suppressions of things which he thought could hurt the power
of the Pope'.[1] Whether such omissions were inadvertent or
not, cannot now be known. Marini did the best he could for
the archives by his lights, over many years of service. But as
he grew old, critical scholars in Germany and France and
Austria did not quite trust what he did. Even in the Vatican
his work was reported not to be accurate. His successor as
archivist (who however had a little axe to grind), once wrote
that the extracts in the British Museum were ill-copied and
worse selected.[2]

In the winter of 1850–1, soon after Marini published the
inadequate book on Galileo, his health failed. He could not
now do the necessary work, which recent events made more

fatiguing. But like the librarian, the archivist by custom had tenure for life. It was not the practice of Rome to put a man into retirement. If he became unfit, the Pope normally continued his stipend and allowed him to live in his house, but gave him a coadjutor, to help him with the work and win the right to succeed to his office when he died.

As his health failed, a coadjutor became a necessity. On 8 March 1851 the Pope appointed a coadjutor. The appointment was surprising. It was the Oratorian Augustin Theiner, already famous as a historian and familiar with the Vatican Archives. He was the first non-Italian to be appointed to take charge of the archives.

Augustin Theiner was born in Breslau on 19 April 1804 of a German father and a Polish mother, both Catholic. He specially remembered his mother's piety, and affection, and the religious way in which she brought him up. All his life he had a special interest in the Poles and other members of the Slav races.

His elder brother Anton raced ahead as a scholar and, while Augustin was still an undergraduate, became (1824) a professor of exegesis and canon law at the University of Breslau. Anton was a young and fiery leader of the reforming Catholic movement in Silesia, and drew his younger brother with him into the assault upon the compulsory celibacy of priests, and the demand for a liturgy in the tongue of the people. In 1828 the two brothers published a work in three volumes on the origins of celibacy.[3] This book did not please authority or escape the attentions of the Roman censors of theological books. But it had the effect of turning the young Augustin into a historian. In these matters the German Catholic world was more free than it became later. The elder brother Anton never submitted; and though he had to leave his professorship, he became pastor of three parishes in succession. As the young Augustin moved closer and closer to the Pope, he never lost touch with Anton; even though Anton was at last excommunicated (1845) and ten years later became a Protestant.[4]

The controversy shifted young Augustin, for a time, away from the Catholic church and into friendly relations with Protestants. He began to react against the faith of his parents and to doubt Catholic doctrine, and to wander, as he himself described it, sadly and sceptically. But he went on with the study of history, turning now to the origins of canon law in the effort to distinguish the real from the spurious decretals in the legal system of the Church of Rome. In 1829 he published at Leipzig a pioneer commentary on the history of canon law.[5] The book established his repute for learning and for skill in criticizing documents.

German scholars took notice of the young prodigy. He refused an enticing invitation to join the faculty of law in the University of Berlin and instead, with a Berlin research stipend, went on his academic travels, to Vienna and then London (where he learnt especially about the Quakers and the Unitarians, 'which are so numerous here'), about the Swedenborgians, and then about the Church of England, which surprised him, and which he could only explain to himself as a survival from a feudal world. Theiner said afterwards that nowhere did he see the fruits of the Reformation in such a shocking shape as in England. In London he attended a place of worship where the preacher kept his children by him in the pulpit, whence during the sermon the children floated down paper darts. He seems to have thought the incident characteristic of English modes of worship. 'The proud individualism of the British has completed and perfected the work of proud and individualistic Protestantism' – this was only one of several harsh sayings after his visit to England. To Archbishop Howley of Canterbury he sent a letter asking for leave to consult the Lambeth Library, and received a courteous assent from the archbishop's chaplain.

Theiner went to Holland and Belgium, then to France, just breathing again after its revolution of 1830. In Paris he published researches into medieval collections of canons which he found, one in London and the other in Brussels. It was afterwards alleged that he became an agent of the French government in 1831, but no reliable evidence has yet been found.

In Paris he was attracted to the group of Liberal Catholics led by Lamennais, with their appeal to Christian democracy. For eight months he lived in the little community of Lamennais at La Chesnaie. In Paris he began once again to go to church.

In 1832 he wrote in France two studies in the ancient and medieval history of Orleans; for which purpose he was helped by the bishop of that city, Beauregard. Here he told Beauregard that once he had thought of ordination, and asked if he might enter the diocesan seminary. Beauregard advised him that it would be better for him to go to Rome. Partly because of Lamennais, Theiner lost the antipathy to Rome which he learnt in the company of his brother. But he had at first no desire to change his country, or to study in a place where he did not know the language. 'Bishop Beauregard said, *Go to Rome.* I should have preferred Siberia!'

Theiner entered Rome for the first time on 1 March 1833 and before the end of the month made public submission to the Church, repudiated all that was censored in his book on the celibacy of the priesthood, and made the Spiritual Exercises at the Jesuit seminary of St Eusebio. He went from one extreme to the other. From being a radical of the left wing in Catholicism, he dedicated himself to the Pope. He now wrote and published, first in German and later in French and Italian translation, a history of his conversion. The new status in Rome lost him the stipend which he received from Berlin for purposes of research.

The History of My Conversion[6] brought him an international reputation, not only among scholars. Some compared it to the Confessions of St Augustine. Pope Gregory XVI henceforth gave him constant support. Cardinal Reisach took him up, and persuaded the Pope to appoint him (though still a layman) professor of Church history and canon law at the College of Propaganda – for he needed a stipend. He worked away among the Roman manuscripts.

Theiner had won the regard and the friendship of Pope

Gregory XVI. The Pope summoned Theiner one evening a week to hear reports on the progress of scholarship and on the problems of the Catholic Church in Germany. At one time Theiner was chief informant to Gregory XVI on the Church affairs of northern Europe.

It was now time to enter a religious order and be ordained. Theiner chose the Oratory, partly because he was attracted to the person of its founder St Philip Neri, and partly because the annalist of the Papacy, Caesar Baronius, had been a member of the Oratory. On 8 May 1839 Theiner entered the Oratory of Sta Maria Nuova in Vallicella, where lie the remains of Philip Neri and Baronius, and where the manuscripts of Baronius are preserved.

For a few years Theiner was uncomfortable in the Oratory. At one point during the early eighteen-forties he came near the point of leaving. The long hours needed by the scholar did not easily fit the monastic way of life with its frequent interruptions for worship and the duties of the community. He was held in his place by a friendship for one of the more delightful and spiritual of Oratorians, Father Carlo Rossi. Rossi was the Oratorian who trained John Henry Newman in that way of life when Newman came to Rome soon after his conversion to Roman Catholicism. Newman's letters show how weighty was Theiner in the Oratorian community in Rome during 1846–7. On Sunday 14 March 1847 Newman and two of his companions communicated at the tomb of the founder of the Oratory, St Philip Neri. It was Theiner who said mass there, and gave them breakfast afterwards.[7] Theiner helped to bring to birth an important new venture in Catholic life.

Baronius carried his Annals to the twelfth century. The Annals received an excellent continuation by Rinaldi, and Rinaldi received a good continuation by Laderchi. Thus the history of the Papacy was brought to the year 1572.

Theiner now asked his superiors for leave to continue Baronius further. His first idea was modest and manageable: to start at 1572 where Laderchi stopped, and carry the history to 1585, thus writing the account of Gregory XIII the reformer of the calendar. The request changed Theiner's future. It pleased Pope Gregory XVI, who gave order that the Vatican Secret Archives should be opened to Theiner, and that he might carry off to his cell in Vallicella the documents which he needed.

Theiner now knew that he had an opportunity such as is given to few historians. He had an inexhaustible quarry of documents which were inaccessible to anyone else, on a subject which the thriving historical world was eager to know. At the age of 36 he reached one of the three or four key-points of European historical studies, when decades of health and energy lay before him, and when he already had a clear idea – clear at least in outline – of what must be done. For this task he was fitted by all his previous training, and by passion for the truth about papal history which can only be paralleled in Lord Acton and Ludwig von Pastor. He was in rapture.

He had a further stroke of fortune. Monsignor Marino Marini at the archives was not learned in German history or the German language, and yet received many enquiries from that historically-minded race. As early as 1836, when Theiner was still a neophyte in Rome, Marini applied to him for help.[8] During the middle eighteen-forties occasional help turned into a regular partnership – the pair of them handling together a 'thorny affair' over documents for the Norwegian government. Marini quickly discovered in Theiner the best of research assistants when difficult questions had to be answered. Gradually they became intimate; even though to the very end of his life Marini was never quite sure how he ought to be spelling Theiner's surname. From 1846 a trouble began to afflict Marini which cemented the alliance more closely. He started the eye-trouble which before the end was to render him almost blind. Inevitably the relationship changed. Instead of Theiner being assistant to Marini, the nominal superior now became increasingly dependent upon his junior. Asked, for example, for copies of medieval bulls, he found that his eyes prevented him reading the registers properly and yet that he must give an answer that day – so he appealed to Theiner to do it instantly.[9]

This intimacy with Marino Marini meant that Theiner's future did not hang upon the favour of the Pope. When Theiner's patron Gregory XVI died in 1846, his licence to use the Vatican Archives lapsed automatically. Marini wrote to Theiner that he would nevertheless continue to release him documents while he sought a new permission. 'Be sure I shall have the same pleasure in giving you all you want when the thing is put in order.'[10] By the following year affection between them was plain on the face of the letters which they exchanged. Marini began to sign himself *Tuissimus Marinius*. And as Marini grew older and iller, he depended more and more on Theiner, until a sad letter of 27 July 1853 – my legs will not take me to the archives, and I cannot meet the Secretary of State's request for a bull of 1496 – will it please you to do it? On 14 March 1851 Theiner became Marini's coadjutor, that is, assistant with right of succession.

Cardinal Angelo Mai, shortly before his death in 1854, was reported to have said of Theiner, 'He is the only man in Rome doing fundamental research. He is a great man, dedicated to the Pope, and the Pope ought to make him a cardinal.'[11] Theiner was not uncontroversial in the Curia. His history of Pope Clement XIV offended, not without reason, the Jesuits whose Society Pope Clement XIV had suppressed. But Monsignor Marino Marini was devoted. He always spoke of Theiner with *ecstasy*, and described to those in authority the *great esteem* and *great affection* which he felt. On the eve of the feast of the Immaculate Conception, knowing that soon he would depart this life, Marino Marini directly proposed to the Pope that Theiner should succeed as prefect of the Archives. Some members of the Curia must have doubted. We know that the Jesuits doubted and perhaps some of them feared. Perhaps others doubted because this was not an Italian, and still others doubted because this was a kind of convert, and still others because they knew the inner fire in the man. But whatever doubts were felt in his entourage, Pope Pius IX

37

confirmed Theiner as prefect of the archives, six days before
Marini died, aged 72, on 21 November 1855. The Pope was
hazy about his archives. He asked Cardinal Antonelli to
get Theiner to make him (the Pope) an index of the documents.[12]

With the office of prefect of the archives went an apartment
in the Vatican. High up a winding staircase in an observatory,
sometimes known then as the Tower of Galileo because Galileo
was wrongly alleged to have been imprisoned there when in
Rome, known now as the Tower of the Winds, the visitor
reached a landing where was a private door into the archives
and a way into the prefect's apartment, with a study adorned
by frescoes, and a loggia with a glorious view beyond Rome
to the countryside and the Alban hills. Theiner was happy
to move from his cell in Vallicella to this room next to the
archives. He hardly ever went out, except to walk in the
Vatican gardens during the afternoon, and refreshed himself
by entertaining visiting scholars on the loggia or in the study.
He was ruthless about time.

The pay was modest. He had his free rooms high in the
tower, and his academic friends were glad because, though he
was still an Oratorian, his new abode got him away from the
varied duties of the Oratorian rule of life and freed his hours.
The stipend was 30 scudi a month, with the addition until 1859
of 12 scudi a month from two of his other minor offices. He
kept a servant to do his cooking and cleaning, and paid a
secretary to copy documents. These payments left little out of
the 42 scudi, and for the rest Theiner lived on a small
inheritance, part of which he used to help the cost of publications. In April 1858 he appealed sadly to the Pope for a
better stipend, saying that he could hardly live in a decent
manner befitting his station.[13] Once, perhaps after this appeal,
the authorities offered him a canonry at St Peter's, with a
stipend of 100 scudi a month. The money would have made
him comfortable. But then he would need to perform the duty
of a canon, and attend long liturgies, choral service twice a day.

Grudging the hours, he asked to be dispensed from the obligation to attend the services, but authority was not willing to treat the canonry as a convenient sinecure. So Theiner preferred the gift of time to the gift of comfort, and refused both preferment and pay.[14] Nothing interrupted his endeavours. Volume after volume, each containing hitherto unknown documents from 'his' Archive, succeeded each other with rapidity, and stood in a lengthening row on his shelves, where he eyed them with a mixture of pride and astonishment. He had a European reputation. Two kings of Bavaria in succession visited him in his tower. The Emperor Maximilian of Mexico climbed Theiner's staircase when he visited Rome to get the Pope's blessing before his fatal expedition.[15] Theiner's birthplace in Breslau was preserved as historic.

Theiner did the traditional work of the prefect like Marino Marini. He provided Europe with historical documents, but more than Marini he knew how to present them with historical criticism. And for the rest, he allowed privileged persons to secure the copies of documents which they wanted, if or when he could find them. Usually he invited them up the 204 steps to the Tower of the Winds, to copy in the study adorned with frescoes.

In the sense in which Europe was beginning to understand the word, he was not an archivist. European scholars now thought of archivists as men who arranged and made easily accessible the papers which they wanted to see. Theiner's papers, by higher order, were hardly accessible, and he did little to arrange what he did not use. The work of a historian was beginning to be hardly compatible with the work of an archivist. This was concealed for a time from Theiner as from everyone else, because so few people were allowed into the archives that it hardly mattered if the documents were ill-ordered. The staff of the archives was still tiny and unskilled.

Theiner was a fine scholar, and gave all his time to scholarship. But he happened also to be head of one of the biggest archives in Europe, which more and more people wanted passionately to be allowed to consult. He needed the qualities of an administrator. We have no evidence that he lacked these qualities. He had no time. One of the Austrians to whom he allowed copies of documents once wrote with an aggrieved air, 'A writer is not suitable for a librarian. He is busy on his own concerns, and sometimes refuses access to materials which he wants for his private use.'[16]

The archives were not in good order. Until the French Revolution they were in fairly good order, as is proved by Garampi's catalogues. But from the move to Paris with the acquisition of many papers from religious houses, they had never recovered. The poet Robert Browning read (1860) the old yellow book which contained the murder story of 1698 which he was to make into an epic poem. He asked in Rome whether they would have records of the case, and was told they could not be found, it was the fault of the French occupation.[17] Browning hinted that this might be an excuse by men who were determined to release no document; and perhaps French occupation may have become an excuse for hard-pressed sub-custodians. But it was no mere excuse. Neither the equipment nor the money were available to remedy the defect. And Theiner was not the man to see that this tiny staff behaved with the required efficiency. We have evidence of documents taken from one armarium (cupboard) being put back carelessly into another armarium, and so becoming impossible to find.[18] Whether it was the inheritance of French disorder, or the tiny staff available, or the failure of Theiner to be very concerned, catalogue revision made slow progress. The similar revision in the Vatican Library was almost as slow.

Theiner performed the customary duty of the Vatican archivist; that is, to keep the documents secure from the world, and to present to the world what it was good for the world to know. Theiner's fame, and Theiner's documents, kept telling the world what a marvellous collection of historical documents he controlled. And still no one might enter the archive under pain of excommunication, and no one might freely see catalogues. They might ask Theiner for what they wanted. They might only get it if the Pope or the Secretary of State approved, and then only if Theiner could find what they needed.

He found a lot. As Theiner became more famous and more established, he acted more freely towards his clients. Men in London and Paris, Berlin and Vienna, repeated Theiner's name. This European stature allowed him an independence which Marino Marini had not possessed. On the letter of rules about admission he was usually precise, and on sensitive areas he refused to co-operate. Though he accepted the usual fees for copies, he was unbribable. His sense of independence grew. He was unusually helpful to an agent of the Norwegian government, Peter Andreas Munch, who was the first to study a whole series of papal registers; and to a recent Catholic convert Hugo Lämmer, who for the first time used the reports of nuncios during the German Reformation.[19]

As Theiner's stature grew, he took wider freedom. And his attitude to one sensitive area – the trial of Galileo – began to change.

Whenever applications came for copies of documents from the Vatican Archives, the applications went to the Secretary of State. Of the various qualities needed for an effective Secretary of State, Cardinal Antonelli possessed only one, promptitude in business. He always referred these applications at once to the prefect of the archives. Sometimes the applicant came away satisfied, sometimes vexed. If he knew the single document that he wanted, or even series of documents, he would probably be allowed to make copies in Theiner's room up the Tower of the Winds. If he wanted to see a whole series hoping to find he knew not what, he was likely to be disappointed. Julius Ficker tried in 1854 and fiercely complained that he was given access under such narrow conditions as to make access useless.[20]

Three or four years later we find two interesting letters of advice from Theiner to Cardinal Antonelli.

The first gave his opinion on an application from the Austrian-protected Kopp. They show the state of mind which still ruled the breast of this scholarly prefect of the archives.

Kopp wanted to use volumes as he liked, not only copies of documents which he specified.

Theiner to Antonelli, 22 October 1857:

...If this privilege is granted, we shall see in Rome half-educated writers and enquirers of every type, Protestant and infidel as well as Catholic. They will come with a special aim into the immense treasures of our archive, all under the protection of some government or other, alleging the precedent of Kopp. Publishers will pay large sums to authors who will fetch them documents from the Vatican Archives. Under the pretext of advancing Catholic scholarship they will really be out for money. The Vatican Secret Archives would soon lose its lustre, its prestige, and all its importance...

Theiner undertook to do all he could for Kopp, but 'in the normal way'.

Shortly afterwards Prince Buoncompagni asked if he might see the papers of Galileo's trial. He applied to the Secretary of State, Cardinal Antonelli. As was his rule, Antonelli referred the application to Theiner. The letter of advice from Theiner (30 June 1858) runs thus:

I have re-read more carefully the famous trial of Galileo. I am even more convinced that it is inexpedient to allow it to Prince Buoncompagni. Its language is very simple and frank. This frankness is today hardly intelligible, and could give occasion to critics.

This was the reason why, on my advice, Mgr. Marini did not publish all the decrees in full, in his book *Galileo and the Inquisition*, so that they were not exposed to evil interpretation by the malicious. Among the decrees is the one which Prince Buoncompagni wants, and though framed in very innocent language it is always susceptible of a sinister interpretation: – 'Galileo was told, he should speak the truth, or he would be led to torture. Galileo replied, I do not hold, and did not hold that opinion, etc. *For the rest, I am in your hands, do what you please.*'[21]

It was a simple threat of torture, but Galileo seems to have believed in the threat. What weapons would this text offer...?[22]

The statesman, or the apologist, in Theiner conquered the historian.

The historian in Theiner never quite conquered the apologist. But something happened to change his mind. The next important application about Galileo came nine years later and received a different answer.

Many unknown reasons might be guessed for the change in Theiner's attitude to the Galileo papers. But the ultimate reason was the appearance in the forefront of European argument of the controversy between science and religion. This happened in the eighteen-sixties, not chiefly because of Darwin, since it would have happened without Darwin. May 1864 was the month when *The Times* first printed a leading article on the subject of science versus religion; and often the leading articles of *The Times* make an index of the time when a controversy is inescapable among the educated.

When all over Europe men argued geology versus Genesis, or reason versus faith, or enlightenment versus obscurantism, Galileo's trial was an important part of the argument. It was the classic case where ecclesiastics stopped scientific research. Of course the trial had often been used in this way. But in the eighteen-sixties it acquired exceptional force through the contemporary context. In the English language Draper published a book, dubious as history but powerful as propaganda, in which Galileo was used as a thick stick to beat the obscurantism of the Roman Catholic Church. In France Dr Parchappe published (1866) a book which declared that Galileo was probably tortured, that Marino Marini *touched up* and *mutilated* the minutes of the trial, and in any case the accuracy of the Vatican manuscript was suspect. The French historians awoke to the battle. The editor of the *Revue des questions historiques* wanted an impartial account. He applied to Henri de l'Epinois, and on 23 November 1866 Henri de l'Epinois applied to Theiner, in these words:[23]

I am commissioned to write a fundamental article on the affair of Galileo and the Inquisition, to put in the *Revue des questions historiques.* If you would lend me Monsignor Marini's book *Galileo e l'Inquisizione*, I should be much obliged, and would send it back as soon as I have read it. Then I would like to have a note about the manuscript of the trial-record...to refute Dr. Parchappe's assertion that Galileo was probably tortured and that the minutes of the trial were touched up by Marini...If I had a detailed note on the manuscript, showing whether it is the original or a copy, whether any of it has been erased etc.,...and a note on the nature and object of the passages printed by Monsignor Marini I should be much obliged and would do you all honour. I cannot write on this subject without replying to Parchappe's assertion. Wasn't it in your room that Galileo lived during the trial?...

Henri de l'Epinois, it will be seen, did not ask for a copy of the manuscript, which he probably thought a vain request; only for Theiner's notes on the manuscript. Theiner, reversing his mind of nine years before, now agreed to release all the manuscript for publication, on the understanding that de l'Epinois would seek to clear the Church of responsibility.

De l'Epinois published the first reasonably accurate account of the Galileo manuscript in *Revue des questions historiques* for July 1867. It was not a full transcript, for though he made hasty copies of parts, he was forced to return to France before completing his text. On 10 September 1867 he wrote a revealing letter of thanks to Theiner, which proves that Theiner wished the text to be published.[24]

By 1870 the papers were out. Theiner allowed an Italian scholar Domenico Berti to sit in his room up the tower, copying Galileo texts.[25] Henri de l'Epinois gathered more. Silvestro Gherardi, who fled from Rome in 1849, returned at the end of 1870 to recover the Galileo papers which he saw during the revolution. No more was mystery, except so far as all historical events remain in part mysterious. Galileo was in prison for 22 days, and comfortably treated; the threat of torture was more a ritual threat by archaic formula than a real threat – but whether Galileo knew that the threat was probably nothing but words is not so certain. No amount of publication could prevent the act of that court being for ever scandalous.

The only difficulty that remained was the friction between too many historians all trying to work on the same texts.[26]

This case of Galileo's trial was the most elementary form of the argument between truth and expediency. The documents at last were released, and truth made easier to find. But truth was only made easier to find, not because it was truth, but because it was expedient that it should be seen to be easier to find. This was not a victory of truth over expediency but of one sort of expedient over another sort. In the Galileo documents were texts which malevolent men could use. The past agents of the Church had not behaved well in the Galileo affair. But in an age of science versus religion, where the truth about Galileo mattered, it would be a worse calamity if the present agents of the Church were seen to be suppressing, or were suspected of suppressing, documents which they were known to have under lock and key; and worse still, if scandals were widely believed and could be reduced by disclosing the authentic papers. Theiner was an eminent historian. Henri de l'Epinois's letter of thanks in 1867 proves that Theiner's motive in releasing the documents was not the quest for historical truth, but a desire to help the present reputation of the Church. Ten years before, he found it best for the Church of the nineteenth century if he sought to protect the reputation of the Church of the seventeenth century. Experience taught him that the reputation of the Church of the nineteenth century was better protected by getting the truth about the Church of the seventeenth century. That was an important lesson. It was not yet all the lesson that there was to learn.

4

The Minutes of the Council of Trent

Soon after the Council of Trent ended its third sitting in 1563, Pope Pius IV had the plan of publishing to all the world the full acts. If he had done so, the history of European controversy would have been different. But he died, and his successor would not publish. On reflection, Rome saw that to publish the discussion which lay behind the decrees would lead to argument on the meaning of the decrees. It was better to have the decrees unadorned, part now of the laws of the Church. The Acta, diligently collected by the secretary of the Council, Angelo Massarelli, were gathered into eight volumes bound in leather with gilt edges and deposited for security in the Castel Sant' Angelo. With them were then or later deposited eighteen more volumes of reports and letters. At first the security was not very strict. About the end of the sixteenth century we find men consulting the papers for aid in their discussions.[1] By Massarelli's diligence, no Council in Church history was better documented. But at that date, probably with the intention of silencing unnecessary discussion about predestination and grace, popes consciously adopted the policy of allowing no one to consult these papers. Not to make them available became an established rule of the Roman Curia. Papers were slowly added, under the general heading *Concilio*. By the time of the prefect Garampi in the third quarter of the eighteenth century the number of volumes had grown to 104; by 1940 it was 155.

The rule against access acquired a kind of theological defence, which survived even into the middle of the nineteenth century when it looked peculiar.

Historians have often experienced this truism, that an early, one-sided, clever and popular treatment of a large subject takes the field and thereafter hampers, often for many years, subsequent saner treatment by historians. When Cardinal Manning died, Purcell published a clever and slightly scandalous biography, with such consequences that more than three-quarters of a century later we are still unable to study the Manning archives freely. This was what happened to the history of the Council of Trent. The Venetian Paolo Sarpi published, in Protestant London, his brilliant, partisan, and sometimes excellently based *History of the Council of Trent.* The book enchanted readers and became the authority all over Europe. No later history before modern times could compete. Whether they had better archives or not, whether their judgment was more impartial or not, other historians could not oust a fascinating if at times misleading book from the European field which it conquered on merit, quality of literature and of forceful aggression against popes as well as of history. Though it stood on the Roman Index from 1619, we are told that half a century later it was read by every educated clergyman in Rome.

It must be answered. Rome selected the Jesuit Alciati and opened to him (under odd restrictions against making copies) the Vatican Archives. The work was enormous; Alciati was conscientious; he knew that Sarpi could not be answered by more apologetic, but only by better history; his draft chapters tarried and finally he died in 1651, over the age of 80, with the book half-written. The Jesuit general then appointed a theologian, not a historian, to take over the work; and within five years, now with wholly free access to the archives, Pallavicino published his *History of the Council of Trent* in two folio volumes (1656).

Pallavicino versus Sarpi: if a single symbol could be taken to divide the religion of Catholics from the religion of Protestants, it was the Council of Trent. Two famous histories stated the rival understandings of what happened at Trent. Naturally the history by Pallavicino became canonized at

Rome. It had better archives, far better, than Sarpi. It was
nothing like so easy to read, despite or because of its rhetoric.
It had no chance of driving Sarpi from his European popu-
larity. But for the Roman theologian, who wanted to understand what happened at Trent and why the dogmatic
decrees were drafted, it became canonized. It was the authentic interpretation of what happened. And therefore, more
than once, anyone who suggested that more evidence should
be published from the archives, was met by the argument that
more evidence could only weaken the authority of Pallavicino.
The appearance of Pallavicino's book was celebrated in Rome
as though it was a victory over Protestants. Nothing must be
allowed to weaken its prestige. When Rinaldi, continuing the
Annals of Baronius, wanted archives for the Council of Trent,
this argument was used for a time to deny him access.[2] Rinaldi's volume, when at last it appeared posthumously (1686),
was indispensable to historians.

The Council of Trent was more than a turning-point in
religious history. It was a focus of European politics. Therefore in all the big archives of Europe, and not only in Rome,
lay papers of high interest – Simancas, Vienna, Naples,
Florence, Trent itself, Munich, Mantua, Venice. In the
eighteenth century slowly, in the nineteenth century more
quickly, these collections were bit by bit given to the world.
The strong revival of denominational loyalties and orthodox-
ies after the Battle of Waterloo turned attention once again
to the importance of the Council of Trent. Some of the
archives, inherited in private families, were sold on the open
market. In this way the Englishman Joseph Mendham used
for the first time the letters of Cardinal Paleotti for his
Memoirs of the Council of Trent (London, 1834). Mendham's
attitude over his own manuscripts shows the possessive streak
which sometimes afflicts owners of historical documents. Asked
by an Oratorian father, who was an emissary on behalf of
Theiner, for the sight of his manuscripts, Mendham coldly
replied that 'foreigners' had plenty of manuscripts of their
own without wanting to see his.[3]

Everywhere documents were published – except from the place where the best documents lay. Historians see the past through the eyes of the authors of the archives which they use. Pallavicino – it was later seen as a defect – saw Trent only through the eyes of cardinals then in Rome. But now men were seeing Trent through the eyes of men in Madrid or Paris or Vienna. Pressure built up, that Rome must publish all, or at least more, of the original documents of the Council of Trent.

No project could be dearer to Theiner. He persuaded Pope Pius IX that publication was desirable if not necessary. The Pope appointed a commission with a Dominican cardinal as chairman, and the commission (April 1857) reported favourably.[4] Theiner got the permission which he sought. In 1856 and 1857 he worked in the Farnese archives at Naples and among the Venetian records, then in the libraries at Turin, Milan, Trent, Padua and Bologna. The Grand Duke of Tuscany deposited forty volumes for his use at the convent where he lodged in Florence. In Bologna especially but everywhere he went, he reported enthusiasm for the project, and gratitude to the Pope and to Cardinal Antonelli, the Secretary of State.[5] Naturally he found many documents which Pallavicino did not know. He refused access to others who wanted to see the documents, because he was working on them himself. He refused the biographer of St Charles Borromeo in words which that applicant described as few and resolute.[6]

Cardinal Antonelli shared Theiner's opinion. When he wrote to the Bishop of Trent, recommending Theiner to work in his archive, he said that Theiner was engaged upon a work of high importance.[7]

That autumn the course of the commission did not run smoothly. Some of the speeches at Trent, which Theiner wanted to publish, contained doubtful matter, even of uncertain orthodoxy. The Dominican chairman Cardinal Gaude asked Theiner to insert footnotes to refute what was wrong or explain what might be misunderstood. Theiner's sense of integrity was offended. He rejected such footnotes, and won.[8]

Worse followed.

That winter of 1857–8 the commission, appointed to advise, suddenly recommended that the plan be suspended. One member of the commission, Father Tosa the Dominican, who began by being hesitant and soon was enthusiastic, suddenly turned against the scheme. The commission saw sheets already printed, and changed its mind.

The old arguments were revived: that Pallavicino's history was classic, and must not lose authority. But a new argument, or new form of the old argument, came to the front; the necessity, as Theiner saw, the undesirability, as Father Tosa saw, of publishing Angelo Massarelli's diary.

Massarelli was secretary of the Council of Trent at all three of its phases. He kept the minutes, and wrote as many as seven different diaries of the proceedings, diaries of unequal value. Massarelli's protocols and diaries were necessary to understand the course of the Council of Trent. No other sources, not even the reports of legates to the Pope nor the letters of national leaders or ambassadors to their sovereigns, shed so intimate a light as the papers of this efficient secretary of the Council.

But Massarelli reported what was said. He recorded the differences of opinion, the follies as well as the wisdom of the speakers, the unedifying as well as the edifying. If Massarelli's diaries were published, the decisions of the Council of Trent, sacred in so many minds, would no longer appear the un-challenged expression of a common Catholic mind, but the end of hard-fought debates over nuances of expression. Only the result had authority, not the course of events or utterances which led to the result. The upholders of Pallavicino main-tained that to publish Massarelli could do nothing but weaken the authority of the canons of Trent, as well as the official history by Pallavicino.

This was particularly true of the early debates on scripture and tradition, the authority of scripture, and its canon. In the cold light of finality, the formulas look rigid against Protes-tants. Seen as the end of a long debate with differing opinions, the formulas have more nuance, more flexibility, than any

Protestant hitherto supposed. The examining commission particularly objected to the minutes which Theiner proposed to publish, and had already in proof, of the debate on the canon of holy scripture.

Thus the Dominican Father Tosa, lately an enthusiast, became the main speaker on the commission of enquiry, that to publish was dangerous, or harmful to the Church. He said emphatically that to print these minutes could hand weapons to Protestantism to attack the Catholic Church and the Council of Trent.

By the autumn of 1857 Tosa sufficiently carried the day for the commission to recommend suspension of the plan.

Such a decision would grievously disappoint any historian whatever, who secured approval of a project, believed that the truth of history in this matter could do nothing but good, worked for months in the archives, and found a succession of valuable documents. Moreover, the plan was announced. Men expected it, and eagerly. To suspend it now might hurt the repute in which Theiner was held, as well as appear a further reaction in papal politics. He had already received money to print. Archbishop Hohenlohe subscribed 1,800 scudi, the Cardinal-archbishop of Vienna and the bishops of Hungary agreed to see to publication, the Austrian emperor gave 3,000 scudi.[9]

By character Theiner was less fitted than some historians to bear so heavy a blow. Beneath the lively, friendly, likeable exterior lay the passionate son of the Breslau shoemaker. He had no patience with his critics. To the Pope he accused them of mere panic. He did all he could. He tried vainly to persuade the commission that new manuscripts, expected from Florence, might resolve their difficulty. He forced them to admit that the time must come sooner or later, when Rome would be compelled, 'blushing', to publish the acts of Trent. He tried to persuade Cardinal Gaude to add a new member to the commission, but failed, the cardinal saying that it would appear to reflect on the existing members. Then Theiner prepared a direct appeal from the commission to Pope Pius IX.

He went to the Barnabite, Father Vercellone, whom he respected as a scholar and man of integrity. In strictest confidence he gave him the proofs about the canon of the holy scripture, and begged him 'freely and before God' to say whether the printing could hurt the Church or the honour of the Council of Trent. Vercellone examined the proofs, and said he could not understand why they were afraid – the speeches of the Fathers of Trent were 'exceeding wise' – in his opinion the publication would be very useful to theologians and redound to the glory of the Church – he hoped that Theiner would go on, and offered his help.

Fortified with this opinion, Theiner appealed to the Pope, in a long petition of 28 February 1858.[10]

It is very grievous, he wrote, to see a single consultor interrupt a work which everyone approves, and which would be 'the consolation of the Church and an everlasting monument to the glory of your pontificate'. The motives for the suspension seem to be nothing but panic. Father Vercellone thought that publication could do nothing but good. Suspension will make your own wisdom look shabby among the Protestants. I say nothing of my own misery. I thank God he had let me be ready to go like a lamb. I now and always will resign myself to his will, and that of your Holiness, to my dying breath.

So saying, Theiner asked for an audience with the Pope.

Two months later in April 1858, the commission was still determined to suspend, and Theiner was still trying to work on the Pope. I will not speak, he wrote to Pius IX on 8 April, of my poor person, which is compromised before public opinion in Europe – compromised with the Emperor of Austria – compromised with the Hungarian bishops. How will we Catholics be able to reply to similar tactics on the part of Protestants? Pallavicino will be justified in all parts against Sarpi, and will always remain classical. It will be wicked calumny to accuse me, because I want to publish the Acts, of a spirit hostile either to Pallavicino or to the Society (the Jesuits) of which he is an ornament.

Theiner begged the Pope for a new examination by a new commission. He suggested the names of two possible commissioners – Father Vercellone (of whose favourable opinion he had earlier informed the Pope) and the Dominican Father Gigli. Theiner said that he would joyfully accept the verdict of these two examiners.[11]

He got only part of what he wanted. The Pope made Father Gigli and Father Vercellone into commissioners, as Theiner wanted. They were not however made members of a new commission, but added to the existing commission. This did not make the commission change its mind. Two years later Theiner wondered whether to repay the 1,800 scudi which he was given by Archbishop Hohenlohe for the expense of publishing; and Hohenlohe said generously that he was owed nothing.[12]

The plan to publish the minutes of Trent came, for the time, to a sudden end. Theiner's bulky notes existed, and the printed proofs of part. They were put into store. This did not mean that Theiner lost the Pope's confidence. Pius IX continued to use him into the eighteen-sixties as an occasional adviser on German affairs.[13]

During the winter of 1866–7 an English historian, fatal bird of ill omen to Theiner, arrived in Rome: Acton. He had specially concerned himself with the history of Trent, and was more interested than surprised to learn that Theiner's publication was postponed, as he said, to the Greek Kalends.[14] Acton worked away at his manifold interests, Theiner providing him with copies of documents. Little by little the relationship became, if not a friendship, a strange kind of intimacy, and for Theiner a calamitous intimacy.

Acton in his early thirties was already full of history. He went to Italy to collect unpublished papers from many of the famous archives. What he intended to write was not yet precise – perhaps a history of Papacy. In Rome his reputation already raised doubts. He was nephew to a cardinal. But lately he edited and financed liberal Catholic journals in England, during a time when liberalism and Catholicism looked to the Curia like contradictory terms. He was also known as the favourite pupil of Professor Döllinger of Munich, whom the Curia had begun to fear. Not all Rome was glad to see this able young Catholic scholar. At least one member of the Curia grudged the privileges which he was accorded.

The ageing Theiner was impressed. He found that Acton could give information on subjects which specially concerned him, and that they shared interests in Reformation and Counter-Reformation. He had begun to need an assistant who understood the history of England. For he had collected more than a hundred documents on the Spanish–English marriage of 1623. He proposed a joint venture – he should provide the documents, Acton should arrange for the publication and write the historical introduction. Acton was so flattered that this scholar of an international reputation should want to use him, that he half-suspected an ulterior motive.[15]

On his side Acton found Theiner an extraordinary person, perhaps the most extraordinary whom he met on his travels.[16] Theiner's romantic career as a young man, with an alleged part as an agent to the French government in settling the Breton conspiracy of 1831–2, appealed to the man of action manqué in Acton's breast. Acton found not only an archivist with treasure at his disposal, but a man who cared as passionately as himself for archives, and for the truth to be gained from archives. He also discovered that Theiner admired Döllinger; and even though the admiration was less whole-hearted than Acton could have wished, anyone who professed himself a disciple of Döllinger was a friend of Acton.

This seemed to Acton part of the astonishing quality in Theiner. Here was a man at the heart of the Vatican who did not share, or did not seem to share, the attitudes which loyalty to the Rome of that day demanded. At little dinner parties in the room of the tower where he was host to selected scholars, he could be abrasive. He had his share of German academic pride, and something of that contempt for Italian scholarship which hampered so many Catholic Germans during the middle years of the nineteenth century. Because Pope Pius IX was determined that the Italian kingdom should not rob him of his secular monarchy over the city of Rome, the shibboleth of loyalty to the Pope, in the year when Acton arrived in Rome, was belief in the necessity for a papal state. Acton, who himself wanted the temporal power of the Pope to end, was surprised to find that this high Vatican officer felt happy if the temporal power ended. When he discovered this opinion in Theiner, he thought it a marvel.[17] Soon he discovered Theiner's obsession. Theiner hated Jesuits.

When Theiner published his vindication of Pope Clement XIV, who had abolished Jesuits, he made a breach between himself and the Society of Jesus. In those early days of the rule of Pius IX, the Jesuits were not specially powerful in the Vatican. But as Italian nationalists pressed to occupy Rome by force, and Vatican officers feared red revolution in the streets, and the world of international liberalism watched with a seeming indifference, the Pope knew that he lived in a state of siege. In this state of mind he turned more towards the traditional and dedicated defenders of the Papacy. The power of the Society of Jesus rose, though unsteadily, in the counsels of the Vatican.

Theiner could not forgive – few historians could have forgiven – the sudden stop upon the printing of his Trent. He suspected Jesuit machinations. As he grew older this suspicion or fear of Jesuits became obsessive in his mind.

Acton found a high Vatican official, fervent in affection for the Pope, yet hating Jesuits, admiring (in part) Döllinger, and having little use for the temporal power of the Papacy. It almost looked like a personal self-contradiction. Acton's surprise may partly account for his later harsh judgment that Theiner was a double-dealer.

By nature they were not quite made for friendship. Acton had the easy assurance of the European nobleman. Something about Theiner suggested memories of a past to be lived down, a feeling of guilt which still lingered, a shadow resting since early days upon the mature man and needing atonement. The grandchild of a prince of the Holy Roman Empire was not quite comfortable with the son of a Silesian cobbler. Theiner had a brawny air about him. When he was younger he was believed to have wielded a pick-axe as effectively as any workman in Rome. His manner lacked subtlety and delicacy. Acton was inclined to see in this roughness a cause of the defects, harshness, violence, overstatements, lack of taste, in Theiner's literary productions. He was wryly amused when Theiner gave him a draft preface for their joint work on the Spanish marriage, 'in which he proposed that I should say what a man he was, how truthful, how religious, and how generous to students'.[18] That Theiner could write books in four languages hardly impressed Acton who could use the same four. Theiner was a compiler of documents, a man who rather heaped than mastered archives. Acton decided that he was no true historian. But as a man of documents Theiner elicited Acton's warm regard. Even eight years later, when Acton believed Theiner not to be straight, he still placed him in the highest category, not of historians but of men who gave the world the raw materials of history. He was prepared to write that in this Theiner surpassed even men like Muratori or Mabillon,[19] and from Acton there could be no loftier praise.

One hindrance to friendship lay entirely on Acton's side. He also began to suffer an obsession.

If authority forced Theiner to stop a mighty work on which his heart was set, the same authority stopped Acton from editing and publishing a Liberal Catholic journal which was the most intelligent Catholic publication of that type in Europe. He was strong in Catholic faith and worship, went to confession regularly, married a devout Catholic wife, and was determined that his children be educated as devout Catholics. But he began to take very unfavourable views of the exercise of Roman authority in the past. He started to search the centuries for occasions when Rome behaved iniquitously. The object of this search was not historical. To him Catholicism also meant freedom and toleration. We must unveil the moments of persecution in their horror, unconcealed, so that never again will Catholic authority dare to fall into such wickedness. Acton was far too good a historian to be a pamphleteer or propagandist using or misusing sources to a contemporary moral end. But because he was what he was, the moral end could not but affect his historical judgment.

This concern for persecution and tolerance was not yet a King Charles's head like Theiner's hatred of Jesuits. Acton was younger than Theiner. The concern took some fifteen or sixteen more years to flower; until at the end of his life, when he was a Regius professor of modern history, the undergraduates of Cambridge University said that he had persecution on the brain. For the sake of protecting an institution, the Pope or the clergy, for the sake of the earthly power of a Church, authority concealed evidence; and this evidence must be uncovered, the documents must be wrested from their hiding places, from the housetops we must shout the truth about Index or Inquisition or intolerance; until the new archival study of history acts like a swab, cleansing the Church by nauseating Catholic minds with the deeds of which Christian men were capable when acting on illiberal principles.

Wrest the truth from the archives – but his new-found friend Theiner controlled access to the most important collection. Theiner was a watchdog as well as a historian. Acton admired the historian and by instinct resented the watchdog. From an early moment in their alliance this started to complicate their lives.

But for nearly four years they were colleagues; working together, the young man admiring the old and famous, and understanding his difficulties, the old scholar flattered that an English aristocrat should work on similar themes, and struck by the tremendous drive to research which in those years dominated Acton's heart. The friendship was never free, partly from difference in background – Theiner began German letters to Acton with the words *Your high-born Lordship* – partly because Acton suspected that the rigid rules of the archives were not uncongenial to the archivist, who liked to have the documents to himself, and partly because Theiner, for all his liberties, was a little too papalist for Acton's stomach. Living near the heart of the Vatican for a quarter of a century, devoting every day to the history of an institution at the centre of the past of Christendom, and still with the self-dedication of a convert, Theiner stood in reverence towards the Papacy; a reverence hardly intelligible to the young half-English historian with his assured inherited Catholicism and his intellectual roots in the European enlightenment.

Theiner agreed to give Acton copies of the much-coveted archive materials on King James II of England and the Glorious Revolution. At this point Acton became aware that Theiner was not a free agent. Before he gave Acton these documents he showed them privately to Archbishop Manning of Westminster, to ensure that he could not accuse him of improper communication of papers; and found that Manning was in favour of their publication.[20] In the autumn of 1866 Acton was conscious that the Jesuits were pressing Theiner against the release of documents. He had heard (in outline) how the publication of Trent was postponed.

Acton was not in the least surprised to find people trying to hide archives, he would have been surprised if he found the contrary. But soon afterwards he began to suspect something more ominous: namely that Theiner himself, in printing documents, suppressed passages discreditable to the Church. Within a year or two suspicion became certainty. Theiner tampered with his texts. So far from Theiner being a man struggling to publish truths which his cardinals preferred to conceal, Theiner was as guilty as his cardinals.

Acton did not know it but Johannes Janssen, working in the Tower of the Winds two years before, had begun to form a similar doubt.[21] Acton's suspicion was aroused by a study of the massacre of St Bartholomew. No moment of Church history touched Acton's soul more painfully. The killing of the Huguenots in Paris, and the approval of mass murder by some churchmen, he saw as a terrible lesson of the consequence of intolerance. He wanted to find out how far approval went – whether the Pope knew beforehand, whether he sanctioned the coup, whether the assassinations were premeditated or were the sudden results of unexpected events. In October 1869 his article entitled 'The massacre of St Bartholomew' appeared in the *North British Review*. Naturally the article has not survived the test of subsequent enquiry, but remained one of his best-known essays.[22] Though he already had a body of intelligent writing to his name, he had never before printed an essay which proved its author to be in the first rank among European historians.

The evidence which (in Acton's eyes) damned the ecclesiastics, was contained in the reports of the papal nuncio in Paris at the time of the massacre, Antonio Maria Salviati. He thought that the use of Salviati's reports was the chief originality of his essay.[23]

Theiner printed most of these reports in the appendices of documents which he added to the first of his three vast folio volumes on the pontificate of Pope Gregory XIII.

Anyone who begins to work on Theiner's extracts from the nuncio Salviati is at once afflicted with doubt. Part of Salviati's letters, though only a little part, was printed before in an unexpected place – the appendix to the third volume of the *History of England* (1825–40) by Sir James Mackintosh. Though the continuator of Mackintosh selected so few paragraphs, these few paragraphs contained matter which Theiner's transcript of the letters did not contain. Sometimes these omissions were of negligible interest. But occasionally, and especially to a man with Acton's bias in favour of disclosing what discredited, they staggered.

Salviati wrote a letter to Rome on 24 August 1572, the very day of the massacre. Theiner printed long extracts, Mackintosh short extracts. But Mackintosh had paragraphs not found in Theiner, and even put a shocking passage into italics:

I am as happy as I can be that God has been pleased to promote the good of this Kingdom so happily and honourably, at the beginning of the pontificate of His Holiness; and that he has taken under his protection the king and the queen-mother, who have been able to extirpate the poisonous roots with such prudence, at a time when all the rebels were shut up in their cage.[24]

Theiner left out the passage. His transcription shows no mark that anything is omitted. In his text, however, he drew attention to the existence of those transcripts which Mackintosh printed.

Therefore anyone, working on the massacre as a historian and interested in Salviati's reports, must want Theiner's text to be checked. Thus dawned the suspicion about Theiner which henceforth perturbed Acton.

He knew that a check was possible.

Sir James Mackintosh was in Paris during Napoleon's Empire, and worked in the archives. Then or later he found copies of Salviati's letters made by Chateaubriand, and from them made his selection. Acton applied to Paris for the full text of the Salviati letters as copied by Chateaubriand, with notes on whatever Theiner omitted. These copies,[25] which he received before writing his article, are still among the Acton papers.[26] 'I had the means,' he wrote later, 'of controlling Theiner.'[27]

Acton was not yet indignant, partly because his obsession was not yet grown and partly because he still worked with Theiner. A man who writes the history of a Pope will not print all the reports of all the Pope's ambassadors, and will have a different aim in his selection from a man writing the history of a particular event far from Rome. Acton's article on the massacre has a charmingly cryptic sentence about irrelevance, which no reader of that time could understand:

Theiner...omitted whatever seemed irrelevant to his purpose. The criterion of irrelevance is uncertain...[28]

Thirteen years later bitterness swept over him as he contemplated the *conspiracy to deceive*. Among the conspirators he was prepared to name three of the eminent historical minds of the nineteenth century, and first on the list he put the name of Theiner.[29] Another thirteen years after that, he described Theiner as a gross prevaricator.[30]

These harsh judgments were not in the mood of 1866–74. Acton was already critical of Theiner – but not as a manipulator of sources, only as a man who had such affection for popes that unconscious bias led him astray.

The lives of these historians now became entangled with stirring political events, the Vatican Council of 1869–70 and the fall of Rome to the kingdom of Italy on 20 September 1870.

When the Vatican Council met in December 1869, it soon divided into parties on the question of the teaching office of the Church, and the nature of the Pope's infallibility. Nearly all the fathers of the Council believed that the Pope (in some sense still uncertain) was the infallible mouthpiece of Church authority. A sizeable minority, some 150 to 200 bishops, did not want the Council to make a theological definition of this doctrine, because they feared that the conversion of Protestants might be made more difficult, and because they believed it difficult to define in relation to the general authority of the Church. The majority was determined to define it; partly because the age of indifference and secularity and challenge to Christian truth seemed to require that, if they had a successor of St Peter who could speak with a divine authority, this authority should be declared before the face of the world, and partly because Pope Pius IX himself took this view of the matter, and loyalty made some bishops wish to define as he judged right.

The theoretical argument pressed sorest upon the historians. If men started to declare the Pope (in some way) infallible, the historians looked back upon the history of the Church and saw moments when the Pope was wrong, and either inferred that the Pope was not infallible or argued that the doctrine must not be defined in such a way as to cover that error. The leader of the extreme opposition, though not a bishop at the Council, was the historian Döllinger of Munich. In Rome worked two of his pupils, both historians, Acton and Friedrich. The little handful of bishops with a historical training were to a man opposed to definition – Bishop Hefele of Rottenburg, Cardinal Rauscher of Vienna, Bishop Greith of St Gall. One or two of the leaders of the defining party gave the impression that history did not matter. How shall we test an eternal and unchanging truth by the studies of academics who cannot even agree with each other? Archbishop Manning of Westminster, who was specially prominent in favour of infallibility, uttered sentences which certainly sounded antihistorical.

Theiner was a historian, and therefore at this moment uncomfortable. In the division of parties the Pope, and the Pope's men, could hardly think of the other side as fully loyal to Catholicism. In large measure Theiner was the Pope's man. He was not a member of the minority, and had no place in the Council. But in the minds of the majority he was associated with the minority. And they were right thus far, that correspondents from the minority always assumed that he agreed with them when they wrote him letters. He had dedicated an important collection of documents to Strossmayer the Bishop of Bosnia, the most eloquent and outspoken bishop among the leaders of the minority.[31] He was a historian at a moment when historical enquiry was unpalatable. He was a German inside the Vatican at a moment when the German bishops were unanimous in opposing what the Pope wanted. Though he was the Pope's man, he became the Pope's man thirty-five years before, in a less beleaguered city. One of the Jesuits was rumoured to have said, 'Theiner is the only survivor from the early entourage of Pius IX. He must be got rid of.'[32]

The company which Theiner kept was no longer congenial to the Curia. Men remembered the kind of visitor who ascended the long winding stair to sup with him in the Tower of the Winds.

The Vatican of 1869–70 was a different place from the Vatican of 1855. In 1855 Theiner was at home in the air of the Curia. In 1870 he no longer had a natural habitation. One example will suffice: the most unpopular or popular letters of the day were the reports from Rome to Munich, published in the *Allgemeine Zeitung* of Augsburg, under the pseudonym

Quirinus. These letters contained a brilliant pillorying of the majority in the Vatican Council, and repeatedly used information available to no one else among the journalists. As early as January 1870, Theiner decided that Acton was the unknown author. Theiner was in part, though only in part, right. But the important point was the nature of his reaction to the idea that his friend and historical colleague should be perpetrating these scandalous letters. So far from being shocked, he was reported by Acton to be 'thrilled'.[33]

When the Vatican Council opened in December 1869, its mode of proceeding was instantly a matter of controversy; whether the heads of the Catholic states should have been invited, who should have the right to propose motions, how the debates should be conducted, whether a simple majority was enough to carry a motion. Naturally everyone wanted to know how Trent conducted its business. The Curia did not wish the proceedings of Trent to be prominent. For the debates of Trent were conducted with less control than the debates of the first Vatican Council – for one excellent and compelling reason, that the number of persons present at Rome was often ten times the number of those present at Trent. An assembly of 60 may behave as an assembly of 600 may not – that is, if useful business is to be done.

Within the first few days of the Council Theiner received orders not to let anyone see his papers on Trent.[34] The order was not specially directed against Theiner. Another Oratorian, Calenzio, who was also working on Trent, likewise received notice to stop.[35] Not to release even the order of business at Trent was a sign of the besieged stance which prevailed among the cardinals during the last days of papal Rome. Sooner or later the opposition would discover the mode of proceedings at Trent. Even if they had known it in detail since the beginning of the Council, that knowledge could have made no difference to the course of events. From all points of view truth would be better than refusal of truth.

In the spring of 1870 opposition bishops were found to possess the order of business at the Council of Trent. They made use of it in argument. The Curia inferred that the knowledge of the document could only have come from the Vatican Secret Archives. Suspicion fell on Theiner.

And now the rumours of his enemies gathered: he was bribable; let rich Protestants into the archives and took no notice of the rule of excommunication; released papers which he ought not to have released to foreigners, even to an Anglican bishop;[36] gave Cardinal Rauscher the materials with which to write an antipapal pamphlet; communicated the order of proceedings at Trent to Cardinal Hohenlohe; communicated the same to Lord Acton, together with a mass of other material which he ought not to have communicated. As early as 4 February 1870, long before the accusations were directly lodged against Theiner, the pseudonymous Quirinus wrote a fatal paragraph:

Father Theiner, prefect of the Papal Archives, has had parts of the first volume of his Acts of the Council of Trent printed. We find there a *Modus Procedendi*, which secures to the Fathers of the Council much more freedom of action than the present regulations... Theiner has been altogether forbidden, by the management of the Jesuits, to publish his work, and has received the most strict commands not to show the part already printed to any bishop.[37]

How had the Austrian and Bavarian bishops acquired the order of business at the Council of Trent?

When Pope Pius IX accused Theiner in April 1870, he does not seem to have accused him of communicating the procedures of Trent directly. The documents of Trent gave only the final push to Theiner's fall. Acton went so far as to consider that even without the affair of Trent Theiner could not have survived, and that the charge of communicating documents of Trent was 'only a pretext'.[38] Acton was wrong in thinking it a mere excuse. But he was right thus far, that it was not the first grave charge that the Pope lodged against Theiner.

On 12 April 1870 Pope Pius IX suddenly summoned Theiner to his presence. He was excited and angry. He said that Theiner was reported to have taken Lord Acton into the

Secret Archives and given him documents for his use. Theiner denied it with decision, and his denial seemed to make the Pope more excited. Theiner then offered to take a solemn oath that it was untrue. The Pope quietened. But he started blaming Acton – 'he is not one of us' – and Friedrich and Döllinger – and then all the German bishops.[39]

When, therefore, the bishops of the minority produced the Trent procedure, Theiner could not survive in charge of the archives. In Munich Döllinger heard from Friedrich of Theiner's 'very painful situation, suspected by the Pope, and accused.' Acton reported from Rome in a series of laconic letters:

4 June 1870   Expect, any day, disquieting news about Theiner. He will almost certainly be dismissed. Today I was with him and will be tomorrow.

5 June 1870 Whitsunday   The storm at last breaks over Theiner's head...Theiner's friendship with [Bishop] Strossmayer gave them [the Jesuits] the means to stir the Pope to action.

Acton to his wife, undated   My friend Theiner has fallen into disgrace. I have been much with him the last two days. I am going to fish in these troubled waters.[40]

Theiner's fate was decided a few days before 5 June. He was out at a villa in the country, working tranquilly away at the life of Pope Benedict XIV, and received an order to return. He went to the Secretary of State, Cardinal Antonelli, who informed him what was decided; characteristically adding that he wished him well, but was powerless to help. Theiner said he was innocent, but in vain. He was required (4 August 1870) to give up the keys of the archives. They trusted him now so little that they walled up the door which led into the archives from Theiner's apartment in the tower.

He had told the Pope that the bishops of the minority had not got from him the documents of Trent. It is likely to be true. After Theiner's death, Professor Friedrich, by then excommunicated for his resistance to the Vatican Council, declared in the *Kölnische Zeitung* that it was he, and not

Theiner, who gave the papers to the bishops of the opposition.[41] Friedrich seems to have asked Theiner whether he might see the text, and was refused regretfully. In 1871 Friedrich printed at Nördlingen the text of the Trent procedure, which he took from a manuscript at Munich.[42] Probably, therefore, Cardinal Hohenlohe was given the text in this form by Friedrich, and owed nothing to disobedience by Theiner.

But in the same year, 1871, a Canon Ginzel published the Trent order of business at Vienna. This text claimed to rest upon a Vatican manuscript, a copy of which reached the editor by Schulte of Prague. Schulte had it from the Vatican by an intermediate hand. Theiner must have failed either wittingly or unwittingly in his duty – either by consciously communicating and afterwards telling lies, or because he showed the printed proofs to persons in the Vatican whom he regarded as trustworthy in keeping secrets and who were careless, or were less trustworthy, than Theiner supposed. It is not at all likely that Theiner told lies; we do not forget the evidence of Acton, that Theiner could not be bribed.

The story got about, corrupted as rumour corrupts at a distance. In Frankfurt Professor Janssen told his favourite pupil that Theiner broke his solemn oath and sent documents from the Vatican Secret Archives to Döllinger in Munich, and that it was not a rumour because he had the story from the man who copied the documents in Döllinger's house; and that in consequence of this breach of trust the Vatican Archives were to be closed to 'almost everyone'.[43]

Theiner was not dismissed, that is, he retained the title of prefect of the archives though he was no longer allowed into the archives of which he was prefect, except under the same stringent precautions as any other scholar – conditions which pride forbade him to accept. Whether from kindness to an old man who would find it hard to move house, or whether from a sense of the scandal in European scholarship if so famous a historian were dismissed, he stayed in his rooms up the tower, and kept his little stipend of 30 scudi a month.

That confused the public, for naturally they still asked him to help.

I am sorry I cannot help you about Aleander's papers, [he wrote to an enquirer] because I cannot enter the Archive since 5 June 1870, and would not enter even if they allowed me. They have walled up both my entrances for fear that I might get another key made. Everything goes through the hands of a little clergyman of St Peter's who knows nothing about it, and to all enquiries after documents answers, 'It is not in the Archives'.[44]

Men still wrote to him asking for recommendations to Cardinal Antonelli,[45] or a fair wind for their private projects. The world was so hazy about the organization of the Curia, that in 1872 someone from Cognac addressed him a letter as 'Vatican librarian'.[46]

The Pope at first gave him a 'superior' – the Archbishop of Edessa in partibus, Monsignor Cardoni, who knew little about archives and history. It comforted Theiner that Cardoni was a friend. But Cardoni died in 1873 and was succeeded by Monsignor Cristofori, who was blind in one eye and half blind in the other and knew nothing about history. Theiner was grieved that if he wanted to see a manuscript he must ask permission like anyone else, and was resolved never to be so humiliated.[47] But he had little fight in him. 'What am I to do? I am an old man, broken in health. I cannot fight any more ...'[48] He shocked those who thought him anti-papal by signing an address of loyalty by Roman professors to the Pope. After the Italian army occupied Rome in September 1870, the Italian foreign minister Visconti-Venosta went to the Tower of the Winds to pay respect to Theiner. Though he came uninvited, his visit was considered as a further act of treason on the part of Theiner. But he was left in peace. Lord Acton observed his behaviour in adversity and admired.

His consciousness of how his fate had been incurred [wrote Acton] gave to his bearing under misfortune a patience which was not without dignity and grace.[49]

Though Theiner said that he could not fight, he fought with the only weapon to his hand. He continued to prepare to print his documents on the Council of Trent.

Convinced that he was surrounded by enemies, and afraid that men would seize his private papers, and suffering from obsession about Jesuits, he got some copies out of Rome in the summer of 1870. His friends argued that an archivist needed to obey, a suspended archivist could use his matter as he thought fit; that here the truth of history must take precedence over the rule which once he must keep; and that to publish the Acts would meet the wishes of Pope Pius IV, who confirmed the decrees of Trent, and of Catholic theologians and historians since the days of Pius IV. With the aid of friends he deposited the manuscripts at Zagreb, where Bishop Strossmayer secretly undertook the cost of printing. Theiner reduced the original scale of the plan, from a possible seven volumes to two, and thereby sacrificed valuable matter.

In early October 1873 Acton, who believed that Theiner was now too old for the work, was astonished to receive a letter from Theiner telling him in strictest confidence that the Acts of Trent would soon appear. Acton was excited, 'How astonishing is your vigour, and power of work!' he answered.[50] 'May the world long be enriched from your treasure!'

In January 1874 Bishop Strossmayer told Theiner that he must get away from the Vatican, if only for the sake of his reputation.[51]

During the summer of 1874 Theiner travelled to Zagreb to supervise the printing of the Acts of Trent. On the day when he was due to set out for Rome, he wrote a letter to an English divine that his 'work was done' and of his hope 'that a better knowledge of the Council of Trent might hereafter promote the reform of the Church and the reconciliation of Christendom'. The journey in the summer heat, through Trieste and Ancona, was hard on the old man. From Rome he went immediately to Civita Vecchia to gain relief by bathing in the seas, and died there suddenly on 9 August 1874.

When Acton heard of Theiner's death, he remembered the defects of character and scholarship and sent a severe anonymous obituary to the *Saturday Review*. But his epitaph rose above this criticism:

In spite of many faults and shortcomings, Theiner had rendered great services to learning, and so far as learning serves religion, to the Church which he sternly loved. His death leaves vacant among European scholars a place which no one can fill.[52]

Two and a half years later the young Ludwig Pastor, who accepted the story that Theiner was a poor historian who broke faith, called to pay his respects to the grand old man of German history, Leopold von Ranke, in Berlin. He was surprised to hear Ranke talk of Theiner with high praise. He did not mention, perhaps he did not know, that this was generous, for in his controversial heyday young Theiner attacked Ranke with ferocity.[53]

The posthumous edition of the Acts of the Council of Trent was greeted with dismay. It was criticized as a painfully inadequate performance. No loyal servant of Pope Pius IX could welcome evidence which they supposed to be filched from the Vatican Archives. Theiner's old methods came under scrutiny. No Protestant could welcome a book from so fervent a Catholic historian who thought that he demolished the authority of that Sarpi whom they regarded as the only reliable historian of Trent. Theiner added useful matter to the store of historical knowledge. But his critics could hardly look at it fairly and be grateful. They could see only the deficiencies which Acton had long seen, the haste in copying texts, the strange or extreme judgments, and in this case the omissions. In a world which Theiner's person no longer fitted, the old and declining scholar gave too many openings to hostile reviewers.

Theiner's predecessor at the archives, Monsignor Marino Marini, made Europe aware of the importance of the archives without satisfying the hunger of historians. Theiner partially satisfied the needs of the historians and thereby made them hungrier. The ill-starred plan to publish the full Acts of the Council of Trent illustrated the two forces pulling in opposite directions. To publish at all was to add to knowledge and simultaneously to show how much more knowledge was to be won. And the illicit (if it was illicit) nature of the venture, the disreputable atmosphere which finally surrounded it – where a bishop of noble character like Strossmayer of Bosnia must keep secret his part in the printing because the Church needed the truth but it was inexpedient that a bishop should be seen to be helping that truth to light – seemed to delay or brake the rapid forces by which historical evidence was released.

Theiner was in small part the victim of his own character. To be a German historian in the Curia of 1868–9 was in itself a predicament. The Catholic historical critics of Germany led the assault upon the plan which the Curia needed or wanted to execute. An acid critic of the time said that a German in Rome needed to give special evidence of orthodoxy before he was trusted or even before he was reckoned a Catholic. 'The mere word *history* in the mouth of a German acts like a red handkerchief on certain animals.' Though Theiner adopted Rome as home, and Italian as a habitual language, it was said of him that he could not italianize, and that *the original sin of his German origin* hung always about his person.[54] In the Curia he survived from an older, less divided world, and lived beyond the time when he could be comfortable.

But in greater part he was the victim of an age, and of circumstances, over which he had no control. He was a sacrifice offered up in the battle between historians who exaggerated what history could do, and divines who wanted to believe that history was almost nothing to do with their task.

A legend arose that he died out of communion with the Pope. This legend persisted, and came into the pages of a Catholic encyclopaedia. As late as 1975 I was told in Rome that Theiner died out of communion with the Catholic Church. It was not true. There is an early story, of which the truth is almost certain, that Pope Pius IX sent a blessing to his death-bed at Civita Vecchia.[55] The monument over his grave in the Campo Santo Teutonico on the south side of St Peter's (for the expense of which collection was taken by Bishop Strossmayer's chaplain Voršak), has no breath of controversy in its Latin inscription:

> Here lies in Christ Augustin Theiner, native of
> Breslau, priest of the Oratory, church historian,
> prefect of the Vatican Archives, who lived a humble and modest life,
> and died aged 70 on 9 August 1874.

5

The Opening of the Archives

On 20 September 1870 the Italian army forced its way into Rome after token resistance and ended (for fifty-nine years) the papal state. To whom now did Vatican Library and Archives belong? Soon the new government started to appropriate Church property in the city. Were these the archives of the state like the Public Record Office, or were they the letters of a private but sovereign family like the papers in Windsor Castle? Had the Italian army captured the equivalent of the British Museum, or the equivalent of the Lambeth Library? Some Italians wanted the new Italian state to declare Vatican Library and Vatican Archives to be national property, in the same way that it took the Pope's palace on the Quirinal and property of religious orders in the city.

In the first few days (and first few months) after the occupation, wild fears circulated, that the Italians were ready to take over library and archives as national property, or that papalists would try to destroy compromising but precious documents before they fell into the hands of the invader. There were rumours that all the archives were being shipped off to Malta for safety, then it was thought that they would sail for the United States, men expected a raid of troops into the archives to prevent their export.[1] The mood of the time is illustrated by the alleged behaviour of Lord Acton over the *Liber Diurnus*.

In the debates over papal authority inside and outside the Vatican Council during 1869–70, the *Liber Diurnus* was prominent. It was believed to be the daily handbook of the papal chancellery used between about 750 and 1050. In Formulary 84 the authors of the new heresy (Monothelitism) were condemned, among them four patriarchs of Constantinople and Pope Honorius. In this formula, therefore, later popes were believed to excommunicate an earlier Pope for heresy. Hence its importance to the arguments of 1869–70.

In 1645[2] Lucas Holste found a manuscript in the cloister of Sta Croce in Gerusalemme at Rome. He was made aware of another manuscript in the Jesuit College of Claremont at Paris, and prepared to publish an edition. But the censors of the Index refused to let him publish. They were disturbed by the profession of faith demanded by a newly elected pope, who was made to condemn one of his predecessors for heresy. The Paris nuncio was spurred to collect two sets of proofs which Holste had sent to friends in Paris. The censors were probably afraid that the publication would hand King Louis XIV a useful weapon in his war with the Pope.

However, in 1680 the French Jesuit Garnier took the Claremont manuscript at Paris and published an edition. He was summoned to Rome to answer for his misdeed, and died on the way. But five years later the Benedictine scholar Mabillon was allowed to see the Rome manuscript in the monastery of Sta Croce, to print an account, and so make it famous. The age of Enlightenment came; peace with the French was restored; and even Pope Benedict XIII now allowed Garnier's old edition to be issued, though only in limited numbers. There were two other editions during the eighteenth century. So it was well-known to scholars. It appears to have passed from Sta Croce into the Vatican about 1798. But copies were hard to find. It was one of the documents which Marino Marini was specially concerned to retrieve in Paris.

When French troops occupied Rome at the revolution of 1849, two scholars Daremberg and Renan made a transcript of the Rome manuscript of the *Liber Diurnus*. On this basis Eugène de Rozière set out to publish an edition. The Claremont manuscript vanished at the suppression of the Jesuits in Paris. Rozière applied to Theiner, and Theiner did not answer.[3] Whether Theiner failed to answer because he could not find, or because he knew that he would not be allowed to produce it, no one now knows. But evidence appeared that one or two people saw it in Rome after 1849, including two French clergymen. Rozière therefore had to make his edition out of a French 1849 copy of the Roman manuscript and the printed texts of the eighteenth century. He published in 1869, and as the Vatican Council loomed, the *Liber Diurnus* aroused lively interest. At Döllinger's house in Munich over Easter 1870 it was a main topic of conversation.[4] Döllinger believed the manuscript to be of extreme importance for the question of infallibility. But he did not know whether the manuscript still existed.

Döllinger fired Acton with the importance of *Liber Diurnus* in the mighty campaign which they both led to prevent the Vatican Council from defining the Pope's infallibility. Acton asked Theiner for it, but to no avail. Acton, who began to take almost fanatical views about the unscrupulousness of his opponents, suspected that they might easily destroy it as the document which was fatal to their cause.

On 16 or 17 September 1870, Theodor Sickel went to Acton's hotel in Vienna to fetch him out to dinner. In the hotel he was surprised to meet Minghetti, Italian ambassador to Austria, who was married to Acton's cousin. Acton told Sickel that Minghetti brought the certain news that within a few days Italian troops would occupy Rome. He (Acton) had devised an adventurous plan. He would enter Rome with the Italian forces, go straight to the Vatican Archive, and carry off by force the *Liber Diurnus*.

We have no reason to doubt Sickel's story of the meeting in the hotel. Acton's rash plan perfectly fits the man at that moment of time. We are not told how he thought he would be able to find the manuscript which Theiner had said that he could not find. But Acton knew what could happen to archives in a state of political upheaval. He had worked in the Venetian archives not long before the war of 1866 which caused Venice to be lost to Austria; and, just at the change of power in that year, the Benedictine Father Beda Dudík appeared with a squad of soldiers and removed eighteen big chests of historical papers and one chest of earlier manuscripts, together with an 'arrested' Venetian archivist who tried to resist.[5] Acton was well aware that when public order breaks down libraries are insecure.

According to Sickel, Acton went, as he intended, to the Italian forces about to attack Rome. But Minghetti warned them of his coming. They put him under courteous arrest, and kept him there for the few days until order was restored in Rome.[6] Sickel said that he met Acton again in 1873 and learnt of his failure. On Acton's death-bed in the winter of 1901–2 Sickel visited him in Merano and tried to get him to remember what happened. But Acton was near the end, and his memory was blurred.

The letters of Acton make the story hard to believe. Acton went to Rome, but nearly a month after the occupation, arriving on 16 October. A letter to his wife of 17 October 1870 describes how he spent his time.[7] No doubt he intended to save what might be saved, and had the *Liber Diurnus* in mind; but he found the city in no disorder, the library and archives shut, and a wall at Theiner's door. He hoped that the Italian government would make the Pope's library national, and open it to scholars of all nations.

The first years of the Italian occupation of Rome were not years when the campaign to get inside the archives could make progress. Papal Rome was in mourning, functions curtailed, ceremonies bare, choirs silent. To keep library and archives under lock and key was one way of asserting sovereignty; and if, from the political point of view, it made another weakness for the Pope by handing an argument to those who maintained how much more useful these books and papers would be if they were nationalized, that was an argument which the ancient Pope cheerfully gave to his critics. The more difficult the Vatican was of access, the more evidently old rights were asserted against intrusive officers or policemen.

Since the road running just past the entrance to the Tower of the Winds was now a public road, the treasures of the Vatican felt insecure. The six or seven years after Theiner's fall were the years when the Vatican Archives were more tightly shut than at any other epoch. An occasional copy of an occasional document was released by special request if a friendly government applied. Immediately after Theiner's dismissal an extraordinary rumour went about Rome, that the Jesuit father Piccirillo, known as one who wanted to be rid of Theiner, received unprecedented leave to go *inside* the Vatican Archives, despite the rule of excommunication, and work there unsupervised. Men were amazed at the story; 'at other times,' said a comic observer, 'such an event would have been regarded at Rome as a downfall of the heavens or a sign of the last judgment'.[8] Whatever the circumstances which caused this rumour to run about the corridors, it was of no importance. Father Piccirillo wrote books, but not the kind of books for which he would find the Vatican Archives in the least serviceable.

The archives were closed, as if against an enemy – for enemies indeed walked the streets of Rome. At this time the Vatican Archive was called *this unapproachable sanctuary*.[9] In the summer of 1877 a Frenchman thought that he was the first (ever) to be allowed to see anything from the archives. In January 1879 a young German thought that he was the first (ever) to be allowed to see anything from the archives; and a story went round that when he asked for the permission the archivist expressed the hope that this would be the last permission to be granted.[10]

The blank years were not quite so blank as these applicants supposed.

Later in life Lord Acton claimed that he gave the first stimulus to the opening of the Vatican Secret Archives. At first sight the claim is preposterous. After June 1870, for understandable reasons, Acton was not persona grata in Rome. At one point in 1874–5 he came near to excommunication. He never again worked in the archive which during Theiner's last years was the main interest of his life and a chief source of his advance as a historian.

In letters recently made available, Acton from time to time mentioned the name of Stevenson. This was Joseph Stevenson, who worked in the British Museum from the eighteen-thirties, a Durham man by origin, with the simplicity and singleness of mind of the true antiquarian and scholar. In many volumes he edited *The Church Historians of England*. For thirteen years he was also vicar of Leighton Buzzard. In 1862 he resigned his living and in the following year became a Roman Catholic. When his wife died in 1869 he sought training in the college at Oscott and ordination to the priesthood. He was very short of money, and the officers of the Public Record Office persuaded the prime minister (Gladstone) to give him a pension.[11]

The account of Stevenson in the *Dictionary of National Biography* says: 'He was deputed by government, after consent had been obtained from the Pope, to make a detailed examination of the Vatican Archives.' When we know of the fall of Augustin Theiner, and the walling-up of the archives, and the Italian occupation of the city, and the mood that reigned in the Curia between 1870 and 1877, this looks like an improbable statement. The truth is still more improbable.

The strange uncomfortable friendship between Acton and Theiner gave Acton an insight into the treasures of the archives and the chance of re-writing parts of English history with the aid of Roman manuscripts. They both knew that Marino Marini copied numerous documents touching English history, and that these documents were now in the British Museum. But neither of them held a high opinion of the value of Marini's copies. Both saw how much was yet to do. On 15 September 1866, not long before he was due in Rome for archival researches, Acton wrote to the Master of the Rolls proposing that the British government negotiate with the Curia that researches might be carried out in Rome.[12]

The matter hung for three years. When Acton crossed Europe on his way to the Vatican Council in November 1869, the Treasury agreed to modest payments for researches on British history in European libraries. A few days after Acton arrived in Rome, he was told (3 December 1869) that the Treasury sanctioned the arrangement, and that his help was needed. Acton asked for explanation. The Master of the Rolls left Acton, the originator of the plan, in complete charge of the delicate operation of extracting British history from Roman archives.[13] No pay was in question; only the sum of £350 to remunerate Roman copyists.

But then Acton led resistance to the Pope's wishes in the Vatican Council. His name was entangled with the name of Theiner, his reputation fell with the fall of Theiner. Acton's control of the plan became a liability if the British government wanted documents from the Vatican Secret Archives. For a moment it was almost like inviting Luther to gain them access to the papers of Pope Leo X. This difficulty was not perceived, either by the Public Record Office or by the Treasury. As late as 17 January 1871 the Record Office asked leave from the Treasury to continue the arrangement; and as late as 25 January 1871 the Treasury gave that leave.

No one enlightened them what conditions were like in Rome. This was fortunate. For they authorized a proceeding which looked as though it had no chance of success, and discovered success beyond expectation.

A year after the Treasury authorized under the direction of Acton researches which Acton could never undertake, the Public Record Office at last perceived that someone else must be asked, and that they knew the obvious man. They remembered the existence of Stevenson – a trained palaeographer, true scholar, recent convert to the Church of Rome, who sacrificed much for his faith. Hardy of the Record Office wrote to Stevenson that the government proposed to employ him to make transcripts of documents in Rome provided Lord Acton should have no personal objection.[14] On 27 February 1872 Stevenson, not without scruples, accepted the mission. No pay was provided, only the £350 allotted earlier to Acton. Hardy was almost too conscious that the Treasury would not consent to another penny. Stevenson's superior at Oscott hardly thought the plan important, for he refused to release Stevenson until he had finished coaching a young man for a routine examination. Lord Acton declared this mission to Rome to be 'perfectly idle and irrelevant'.[15]

Stevenson arrived at Rome early in July 1872; thinking it foolish to come then because the important libraries were closed until November, but obeying the behest of the Public Record Office. He intended to gain access, if he could, to the documents of the Vatican Archives, the Vatican Library, and other Roman libraries, beginning with the reign of King Henry VIII. He carried with him several letters of recommendation – Archbishop Manning to Cardinal Antonelli, Bishop Ullathorne of Birmingham to Cardinal Pitra, the President of Oscott to Archbishop Howard and Monsignor Stonor, these last two being the two influential Englishmen resident in Rome. The Foreign Office instructed Jervoise, the British chargé in Rome, to do whatever he could to help.[16]

The Master of the Rolls gave Stevenson printed instructions which he could show to the Roman authorities: that he was to begin with the reign of Henry VIII and secure copies of documents issued between 1509 and 1547: that the bundles of nuncio reports would probably be very interesting: that the transcripts should be made in full: that he should not order copies of any documents already printed by Rymer, Theiner, or any other known collection: that he should send a report on his work every six months: that after Henry VIII he should proceed to later reigns: and that when he had finished the reign of James II he should go back to the Norman Conquest.[17] This last sentence shows that the officers of the Public Record Office had no idea what they asked him to undertake. They were as hazy as the Pope when he asked Cardinal Antonelli to get him an index.

Wherever Stevenson went, men poured cold water on his plan. At the English College they advised him that he must work slowly towards gaining access. At the Gesù the Jesuits expressed their surprise at what he wanted to do, and said that a request to make a general search in the archives was un-precedented. 'The impression is,' wrote Stevenson to Hardy (1 August 1872), 'that we shall fail; I cannot but see this. Still, I am not discouraged...' When at last he secured an interview with Cardinal Antonelli, he was told that the request 'was unprecedented, that no one had as yet obtained such a privi-lege, that the documents were of the most private character and touched upon matters of extreme delicacy and import-ance'. Antonelli then made his customary courtesy to such applicants, that he 'would take the matter into consideration and promote it as far as he fittingly could do so'.[18]

Three weeks passed and nothing happened, that Stevenson could know. The Vatican Archives show that the business-like Cardinal Antonelli at once consulted the archivist Debellini. Debellini reported to the Cardinal that it would not be difficult if Stevenson worked at the Archives; in 'the present state of rearrangement we might not be able to find him everything that he wants. He ought not to work *in* the Archives as the letter of Archbishop Manning seems indirectly to ask. We have an established custom that for the integrity of documents no one should work except under supervision. Such supervision is at the moment difficult because the staff consists of two persons and both are engaged on the rearrangement.'[19]

Stevenson was impatient that he heard nothing. At the end of September he went again to Antonelli and was told that nothing was decided. He waited anxiously for a letter which did not come. But on 10 October 1872, after the time of the post, Monsignor Stonor came to his apartment on the fifth floor of 24 Via Vittoria to tell him of a message from Cardinal Antonelli: he was to be admitted to the archives, 'on the express authority of the Pope' and under 'an arrangement to be made with the archivist'.[20]

Next morning Monsignor Stonor took Stevenson to the archives to meet Signor Debellini. (The official prefect was still Theiner, who was not allowed into the archives, Theiner's official substitute was Archbishop Cardoni who was ill and did not go near the archives; Cardoni's sub-archivist was Debellini.) He began work on Saturday 19 October 1872.

He received every courtesy, was shown the catalogues, allowed to ask for whatever documents he needed, and to make copies. He was not aware that Theiner thought Debellini to be incompetent. The stories about Theiner which he heard in Rome were not to Theiner's credit.

Stevenson soon realized 'painfully' that he would not get far, amid the mass of valuable papers, by copying everything down in long hand. He asked Debellini whether he and his assistant would help. Thenceforth he made notes of the documents which touched the history of England and Ireland and handed the notes to Debellini. Into each volume of briefs he inserted a large paper with notes on the documents which he needed to have copied, their dates, writers, and first few words; and handed back the volume. Debellini allowed him to work from 10 a.m. until 2 p.m. which was the time of Debellini's dinner. He kept being surprised at the courtesy which he received. Towards the end of November Debellini found him a private room for his work, and Cardinal Antonelli sent over a young priest to fetch documents.

To be the only man working at the Vatican Archives was extraordinary. The quiet ingenuous Stevenson showed no sign of finding it extraordinary. He was excited, but by the materials which he found and not by the privilege. In his report at the end of six months of work, however, (4 January 1873) he mentioned that he was the first ever to gain access to the Vatican Secret Archives. This was not true. But Stevenson knew nothing of the reign of Theiner, or nothing that was accurate.

The official deputy-prefect, Archbishop Cardoni, who was too ill to go near the archives, summoned Stevenson, and was gracious. But on 15 February 1873 Cardoni died and the archives were promptly shut, and Stevenson could do no work there for more than two months. In April Monsignor Cristofori was appointed to succeed, and at once confirmed Stevenson in his privileges, and allowed the work to restart.

Stevenson, and Hardy, and the Master of the Rolls, and the Treasury (which authorized £100 to pay for transcripts on 22 January 1873) were beginning to sense that all was not well. Stevenson was at work, certainly. But no documents were yet forthcoming. London began to press Stevenson. Stevenson began to press Debellini; and was disturbed to discover that small progress had been made in the copying and that this was partly because Debellini could not easily read the old handwriting, and partly because he could not decipher English names which he did not know. Stevenson stopped searching and went back to copying in his own hand letters of the reign of King Henry VIII. He got hold of Debellini's incomplete drafts and filled in the blank spaces. Then he discovered, to his grief and disappointment, the rule that no copies might be removed from the archives unless they were made by one of the Vatican copyists, and therefore he could not get back his own papers.

Just before the archives closed in June for the summer vacation, and Stevenson returned to England, he attended to receive copies of 50 documents – was told that the charge was more than 1,000 lire (£50) but that Monsignor Cristofori waived his claims and that would make it £16.

He had worked in the archives from 19 October 1872 to the middle of May 1873 (with a break of over two months caused by the death of Archbishop Cardoni) and the result was 50 documents at a cost of £16; which Stevenson reckoned as a possible result of one month's work. Not surprisingly the Public Record Office, and the Master of the Rolls, and the Treasury, were not pleased, and began to wonder whether the mission was worth supporting. Someone in the Foreign Office said that they were wasting time.[21]

They were all agreed that better conditions of work must be achieved. Stevenson proposed that Cardinal Antonelli be approached again, to allow (1) that Stevenson's copies be treated as Vatican copies, (2) that they should be attested as though they were Vatican copies, (3) that payment be made from London, and (4) that he be allowed to remove from the archives his own notes of documents which he did not think it necessary to copy in full. Stevenson thought these must be granted if work was to proceed satisfactorily but doubted whether they would be granted. At the Public Record Office Hardy was so angry that he talked of cancelling the mission and publishing the reasons, to discredit the Vatican. Stevenson was hurt, and told a friend that it would have been better for himself if he had never gained access to the archives.[22]

In autumn 1873 they applied again to Cardinal Antonelli, who this time took the extraordinary step of visiting the archives to see what happened. Though he refused to allow Stevenson to make copies in his own hand, Stevenson was pleased at the results of the visit. The occasion was a little more tense because fears revived that the Italian government would confiscate Vatican Library and Vatican Archives, and sell their contents. Stevenson even wrote to his friend John Morris in England, to suggest that if this robbery happened the British Museum should buy 'largely'.[23] Even so, he grudged the slow progress and was continuously conscious of discontent in London. He began to blame Theiner for doing so little to get the archives into order.[24]

But now a young priest whom Cardinal Antonelli sent to help the archivist began to change the conditions of life. He was Pietro Wenzel, whose name is met again and again in the work of eminent historians in the last decades of the century; German by descent but born in Rome and wholly Italian.

Wenzel, the most junior, was the only officer of the archives to survive the changes of that year 1874. In late summer, Theiner died at Civita Vecchia; and although his death could make no difference to what happened in the Vatican Library or Archives, it was felt there as the end of an epoch. In October Signor Debellini died of fever, perhaps, as Stevenson guessed, because his health could not bear the cold in the archives.[25] About the same time Monsignor Cristofori broke his thigh and appeared no more in the archives. To succeed Debellini a Signor Vincenzi was moved from the Vatican Library. But they were getting used to Stevenson. On 20

November 1874 Monsignor Stonor escorted him to see Cardinal Antonelli and then Pope Pius IX himself, who was found to know all about Stevenson's work. Cardinal Manning, thanking the Master of the Rolls for a line of congratulation on his cardinal's hat, said that Stevenson inspired confidence in Rome by his honour and rectitude.[26]

Wenzel the junior, not Vincenzi the senior, was the more important. Vincenzi cared little about the archives and seldom entered. Wenzel discovered his way round the archives, was now the only expert in Rome, and the first, since Theiner fell, to begin to know what they contained. And Wenzel was free, or behaved freely. He poured information into Stevenson, located documents that Stevenson did not know to exist, and allowed him to do whatever he liked – so that Stevenson, to his joy and astonishment, found himself going into any room or floor of the archives, taking down whatever document he liked, copying whatever he liked. He had freedoms which no visitor ever had before, and could never again enjoy. He found this freedom a snare as well as a pleasure. Confronted by unknown papers at every hand, 'the temptation to look over volume after volume is so strong that I fear I have permitted it to captivate me, and I have copied only a few papers. I find now that what I caused to be copied formerly was matter of a very third rate interest compared with that to which I now have access.'[27] He was astonished to find that he had far freer entry to the Vatican Secret Archives than any worker had entry to the British Museum or the Public Record Office.[28] He wrote to the Master of the Rolls in April 1875, 'I am the only one who has admission to the Archives. Several English have tried, French and Germans innumerable, but all have failed.'[29]

So, for a year of this period when the world believed the archives to be shut, and when German and French and Austrian and other English historians complained bitterly against the barriers, an Englishman roamed freely among the cupboards, more freely than any visitor before or after.

For a year he enjoyed his liberty and the help of Wenzel.

But his enjoyment was too mixed to allow him to continue. He had freedom to see, but to get copies was far more difficult because copyists were few and busy. His health found the cold of the archives hard to bear; copying for the English government was tedious when more fascinating matter lay within reach; he began himself to doubt whether the results were worth the expense; and he resented the criticism from London that the outcome was meagre. Stevenson began to lose faith in his work. During 1876 he decided that he could no longer endure.

He did not wish to leave the archives, only to leave the service of an ungrateful British government. The difficulty was the old difficulty, that only representatives of a government ever gained access, and how could he gain access if he ceased to be a representative? In October 1876 he asked Cardinal Manning to petition that he might study in the archives for 'private purposes', and met blank refusal, from Manning's conviction that if he asked for too much he would lose all.[30]

But, unknown to the Public Record Office, Stevenson was already using time for 'private purposes'. Given unlimited freedom by Wenzel, he could find priceless documents for friends who needed information. His close friend the Jesuit John Morris was working on the reign of Queen Elizabeth. In April Stevenson sent him transcripts of Vatican documents; not merely sent him transcripts, but asked him (in fulfilment of the contract) to pass them on to the Public Record Office *except* (not in fulfilment of the contract) those which in the opinion of Morris should *not* be in the Public Record Office.[31]

Thus Stevenson in his turn, like Theiner before him, like Cardinal Antonelli, like Pope Pius IX, began to exercise a censorship on the documents of the sixteenth century. We must not think of him as won to the creed that truth takes invariable precedence over expediency.

On 22 September 1876 he wrote to the Public Record Office resigning from the coming Christmas Eve. The authorities in London believed in the mission sufficiently to appoint a successor instantly, as they found a suitable man ready to hand.

But they were perturbed, and asked a lot of questions, when they found that Stevenson continued in Rome three months after his resignation, still working in the archives, but for 'private purposes'.

Stevenson found a means of support, and a way of continuing. His Catholic friends in England realized that he was finding documents important to the history of the Catholics in England. They approached the Duke of Norfolk, who agreed to help with money. Cardinal Manning also agreed to help. They needed to persuade the authorities in the Curia that this student, who no longer represented any government, might continue in the archives as a private person. His friends saw that if he was given such extraordinary privilege openly, and the privilege became known, the archives would find it hard to bar entry to any private person. They therefore tried to persuade Cardinal Franchi of the Congregation of Propaganda to persuade the Pope that Stevenson ought to be taken unpaid into the staff of the archives. Monsignor Stonor went to see the Secretary of State to ask that Signor Stevenson be made an *extraordinary employee* of the archives. He argued that Stevenson was *very capable* at this kind of work and was a great help to the official archivists. The Secretary of State did not think it necessary to have Stevenson as an employee, but agreed to continue his extraordinary privilege to work in the archives.[32]

Meanwhile William Henry Bliss, Stevenson's official successor from the British government arrived in Rome on 2 January 1877. He had letters in his favour from Cardinal Cullen and Cardinal Manning. Nevertheless he was shocked to find that he would not be accorded the privileges accorded to Stevenson.

The happy time was over when Father Wenzel, junior in the archives, let Stevenson roam. The reason was the death of the Secretary of State, Cardinal Antonelli. The Cardinal ruled the Vatican with urbanity for quarter of a century, and the death must mean change: a new Secretary of State, a new archivist, a new sub-archivist. The new Secretary of State was

86

Cardinal Simeoni; governments hoped that the policy of the Vatican would change, and that he would be more liberal than Antonelli; their scholars applied for leave to work in the Vatican, so many that Simeoni found it prudent at first to refuse all lest he must concede all. 'However,' wrote Stevenson to his friend Estcourt, 'we may hope for the best.'[33]

On 13 January 1877 Bliss was granted an interview with Cardinal Simeoni, who shattered him by saying that Stevenson was still working in the Vatican and another Englishman could not be admitted. 'All that he had heard of my mission was from Monsignor Stonor, and the letter I had brought from Cardinal Cullen. I then said that Cardinal Manning had assured me on 26 December last, when I saw him in London, that so long as I did nothing to forfeit the confidence placed in me I should enjoy the privileges accorded to Mr Stevenson. He replied that he knew nothing of Cardinal Manning's application, and the entry to the archives could only be granted by the Pope, who had said he would grant no more admittance. . .'[34]

The fact was, the Cardinal was preparing to admit one, perhaps more, foreign workers into the Vatican Archives, and could not allow Bliss special privileges which must be denied to others. The unique British privilege ended. Also, the chief archivist changed. The new keeper was Monsignor Rosi-Bernardini, stuffiest head of the Vatican Archives during the entire nineteenth century.

But a little movement could be observed. One nation was prominent in Rome by its scholarship: Germany. Ever since Niebuhr and Bunsen early in the century, they led the Archaeological Institute which they did most to found. In theory the Institute was international, in practice hardly anyone but Germans sat upon the committee. In 1871 the German government made it dependent on Berlin.

In the decade after 1870 this German predominance altered. Perhaps the fall of the German Theiner contributed a little. What was important was the change of political attitudes in the Curia. Always the approach to the archives had been authorized through government. But from 1872 the Prussian government, which was hard to disentangle from the German government, began its persecution of the German Catholic Church in the *Kulturkampf*. Meanwhile the French government, its international power shattered by the Franco-Prussian war and its attitudes made more Catholic by reaction against Communists, suddenly became once again, for a very few years, the favoured son of the Pope, as the only possible protector of the Pope against the attacks of the Italian government. The French ambassador to the Pope, who lived in the Villa Borghese, was a man of influence.

In the years when Joseph Stevenson ranged the archives with freedom, the French set up studentships in the Villa Médicis for selected young men who would afterwards go to the French Institute in Athens. This freshman-year for students of Greece began in 1873; in the following year, now in the little Villa Mérode on the Quirinal, it became the Ecole archéologique de Rome; and in the end of 1875 it gained its present home, its first independent director, and its present title, the Ecole française de Rome. Several of its students were of rare quality, like Louis Duchesne and Eugène Muntz. In theory it was dominantly an institute of archaeology. But its new head, Auguste Geffroy, was a historian, and consciously pursued medieval history as well as archaeology. For a few years he still needed to defend himself to Paris against the charge that he allowed the school to aim at other themes besides archaeology.

His arrival coincided with a new home for the school, on the second floor of the Farnese Palace. It belonged to the ex-king of Naples, but was occupied only by a manager, the ex-nuncio to the kingdom of Naples, two servants, and some squatters, among them a duke who claimed to be a friend of the ex-king of Naples. The government of France rented the entire palace, partly for its embassy to Italy and partly for its school, though it took several months to eject the occupants. When Geffroy at last moved in, he lived for several months in discomfort.

Geffroy knew he must get inside the Vatican Archives, and

did not know how an Englishman roamed among its shelves. He started with the handicap of sharing a palace with the French ambassador to the Italian government, for the Curia did not like communications with the Italian government. But he was a man of tact and good sense. He began secret negotiations with the new Secretary of State Cardinal Simeoni – secret at Simeoni's insistence, lest others like Germans start to demand the same privileges. The negotiations lasted for more than six months, till 29 May 1877. He had the leave of the Pope and the new Secretary of State. He still needed to conquer the new archivist Monsignor Rosi-Bernardini, who would let no one into his archive under the old rules. Monsignor Rosi said *No one goes in and nothing comes out.* He not only said this once but kept on repeating the axiom. The difficulty was only in appearance. They persuaded him to find, not a room next to the archives whither manuscripts might be brought, but a seat in the reading-room of the Vatican Library, by the window alcove which was nearest to the archives. This seat in the library was reserved for a French worker at the archives. But no one else was to know of these arrangements.

The man sent to occupy the special seat in the Vatican Library was Elie Berger, the son of a French Protestant pastor. He had made the first suggestion to Geffroy that the French should negotiate to get inside the archives. The French limited the application to the registers of Pope Innocent IV, which were brought to the special seat by the library window. This seat soon became known to other workers in the library as the French table.

Berger was a Protestant, though at first this does not seem to have been known, and an unassuming man who like Stevenson won the affection of the archivists. To keep out Austrians and Germans, Berger had to promise to say nothing about his studies in the far corner of the Vatican Library. Towards the end of this time French scholars noticed glances, which they suspected of envy, towards Berger's table at the window, and fancied that the secret was slipping. But the secret did not slip. The German Ludwig Pastor gained permission in January 1879 to do what Berger had done for eighteen months, and believed that he was the first to gain such a privilege.[35] Meanwhile other scholars, like the new agent of the British government Bliss, must be content with old-fashioned methods, asking for a particular document and receiving from an archivist a copy at no low fee.

The French success was an important little moment. They were given leave to work at registers of the thirteenth century. A visitor was given officially – for Wenzel's treatment of Stevenson was unofficial – unrestricted access to a restricted but substantial series of volumes. The old system, which under Theiner became so absurd, of an uncontrollable selection of documents by an archivist, was abandoned formally.[36]

For several months Bliss continued to worry that he could not do better. His relationship with Monsignor Stonor was chilly, and the chill was no help. But slowly he began to manage the new system. During 1877 and 1878 the pace was as slow as Stevenson's or slower. Then copies came in a rush: 441 for the first six months of 1880, 266 in the second six months, far more numerous than Stevenson ever obtained. But this was due to another change of management.

Monsignor Rosi-Bernardini was stiff and precise. Though he had the merit of efficiency, the Germans and French regarded him as a pedant. The papers were not so easy to get. Even if a student got leave from Pope and Secretary of State to see selected documents he still needed to conquer the resistance of Monsignor Rosi.

Moreover, Rosi did not treat his customers with the old flexibilities of Marino Marini or Theiner. He insisted on the rule – that is, to look carefully through all the copies before anyone took them away. Consequently his private rooms were littered with piles of other men's papers which he had not time to peruse, while historians outside grieved at the delay. When at last he looked over them, he made excisions which clients regarded as senseless.

The frustrations of that age may be illustrated by an article printed in the *Allgemeine Zeitung* of Augsburg on 17 May 1880

(p. 2010). It summarized an interview between a learned German and a cardinal reported to be liberal, in which the German sadly recounted the failure of all endeavours to get inside the Vatican Secret Archives. Then the author of the article passed to bitter complaints. The effect of the interview was this: 'The Pope has good reason to let no one inside the archives. There are many things which we do not want published. If the Secretary of State and the Archivist allow certain exceptions, they do so with the greatest precaution and under strict control.' This, said the author of the article, is the attitude of the authorities who control a most important collection of archives for medieval and modern history. Everywhere else the doors are wide open. In the Vatican they are shut tight; and they have got more shut during the last twenty years.

This was only one of many attacks in those years. Why are these archives closed? – they must have dreadful secrets to hide. Rumour supplied a disgraceful secret or two. The reputation for secrecy became a proverb, and it was half-believed that the dragon-guardians refused to produce their treasures even when the Pope commanded; a half-belief not discouraged by the conscientiousness of Monsignor Rosi. It was half-believed that there were no catalogues, and that this was intended, so that papers were difficult to find and archivists ruled as despots.

In February 1878 Pius IX died, and Leo XIII was elected.

Like most of the cardinals of Pius IX, Leo XIII was a conservative, and he ruled a Curia whose members were more conservative. He was not specially equipped in theology, and in history was not especially interested. But he wanted to diminish the sores of irritation which Pius IX left between Rome and almost all the governments of Europe. He wanted also to encourage those broader streams of Catholic thought which in the last years of Pius IX were disreputable.

The prefect of the archives was still Monsignor Rosi-Bernardini, and so long as he ruled, nothing changed. In the summer of 1879 the conditions were changed dramatically.

In May 1879 Pope Leo XIII made several new cardinals, among them two whose elevation was momentous for the study of history – John Henry Newman, and Josef Hergenröther. Newman, quiet, remote in his Oratory at Birmingham, was the one man in Europe whose mind struggled with the predicaments of Catholic faith in a modern world of 'scientific history'. Hergenröther was professor of church history at Würzburg, where he was one of the worst lecturers in Germany, droning away behind a high pile of books, with small capacity for selection, and incapable of communicating any feeling for the past as alive. These defects as a teacher did not prevent him being important in the Catholic scholarship of Germany.

The events of 1870–1 spelt calamity for the Catholic schools of history. Germany was the one country in the world where Catholic historians competed on equal terms with Protestant historians. But in 1871 Döllinger was excommunicated, and the majority of professors of history in German Catholic universities followed him out of the Roman Catholic Church. These events almost destroyed the reputation of Catholic history in Germany; damaged the progress of research; and made it hard for universities to fill their chairs worthily.

Hergenröther, though formerly one of Döllinger's pupils, remained faithful to the Pope. No one could question his learning or capacity as a historian. He was one of the few surviving anchors of the Catholic historical schools. More by name and writing than by teaching or influence upon pupils, he helped the difficult process of rebuilding 'scientific history' in the Catholic colleges of Germany. His choice as cardinal was as encouraging to some German Catholic intellectuals as the choice of Newman was encouraging to English Catholic intellectuals – not however to all the German Catholic scholars, some of whom regarded him as too ultramontane to be counted a sound historian.[37]

Monsignor Rosi died suddenly on 6 June 1879 – to Pastor's

alarm, for Rosi had a 'mountain' of Pastor's copies, waiting censorship in his room. Four days later the Pope nominated his new cardinal, Hergenröther, to be prefect of the archives.

The appointment was courageous and excellent. Apart from all other considerations, Hergenröther was better placed as an archivist than as a professor – unless the saying, once made about Theiner, be accepted, that a writer is not suitable as a librarian. His name restored to the headship of the archives that European repute for scholarship which the office lost on the day when Theiner was forced to surrender his keys. And more, he was a cardinal. To place a cardinal in charge of the archives was to raise the importance, and probably the influence, of the prefect. And this cardinal, however monotonous as a teacher of history to the young, was historian enough to know that the archives ought to be open.

On 10 June 1879, the very day when the news of his nomination spread round the Vatican, Cardinal Hergenröther asked the young Pastor to draft a memorandum about the archives – 'how they could be valuable for the writing of history' – 'for,' said Hergenröther, 'the Pope wants books published that are thoroughly based'. Pastor's sigh of ecstasy can almost be heard from the pages of his diary. 'I am sure,' he wrote, 'that the nomination of Cardinal Hergenröther as archivist marks a new epoch for Catholic historical writing.'

Later in life Pastor was inclined to claim much consequence for the memorandum which he then drafted. It will not do to exaggerate its importance. Pastor was still young and unimportant. The policy which his memorandum advocated was decided upon before authority received his memorandum. Only three days after Pastor's interview with Hergenröther, the Austrian ambassador at the Vatican wrote to his foreign minister in Vienna, that the Pope wants the archives to take their place with other European archives of similar stature, and to make access easier; and to this end has asked Cardinal Hergenröther to draft a scheme for a better organization of the archives, and to lay it before him within six months.[38]

This enlightened plan was easier to announce than to execute. Most members of the Curia were men of Pius IX, and stiffly against any opening of the archives. Hergenröther was a true scholar. But he was also a German; and the appointment of another German would have roused misgivings in the Curia even if they did not remember Theiner. Much would depend on Hergenröther's colleagues. And, perhaps under pressure from members of the Curia, the Pope soon diminished Hergenröther's freedom of action by creating a new post of sub-archivist, appointing an Italian to the post, and selecting a man known to be an intimate friend of the Pope himself: Monsignor Pietro Balan, installed into his office by Cardinal Hergenröther on 11 November 1879.[39]

Pietro Balan came of a modest family in the north and became a leader of the Catholic political right in Padua, Turin, Venice and Modena; writing articles and pamphlets, editing very conservative newspapers, defending the Syllabus of Errors, and in his spare time publishing works of history which were less than impartial (including two volumes on a life of Thomas Becket, and three volumes on Pope Gregory VII). He was a lively propagandist and fierce controversialist. From 1875 he began to publish at Modena a *History of Italy* which reconstructed in polemical and readable mode the tale of the revolution as it turned against the Church. He was far from being unlearned. But for the purpose of a historian his learning could not compensate for the one-sidedness, the sweeping judgments, and the habit of the journalist.[40]

How he came to be a friend of the future Pope Leo XIII is not known. But he became an intimate friend. Leo took him to the Conclave of 1878 at which he was elected Pope. No doubt Leo needed to find a harmless post in the Curia for his firebrand. No doubt Pietro Balan, engaged on his *History of Italy*, welcomed the access to the archives which the new post gave him. He had the merit of wanting other men to use the archives for good purposes. But he was not wholly suitable. He did not truly care about learning for its own sake, was increasingly eccentric in his personal habits, and had a dominating personality. Moreover, he was far more Italian than Hergenröther, and closer to the Pope than Hergenröther. Since Hergenröther's appointment the archives had a cardinal as their head. It was soon clear that the cardinal did not rule. The sub-archivist gathered power, and left Cardinal Hergenröther to go on with scholarly work. If Balan were absent the scholars found it difficult to get what they wanted, or do any work, or discover what the archives contained.

Whether it was Hergenröther, or whether it was Balan, or whether it was Pope Leo XIII, or whether it was all three, the door to the archives began slowly to open. At first (during 1879) they seemed merely to have returned, back behind the last difficult years, to the state of affairs under Theiner, though without the haphazard liberality of Theiner – that is, specially selected persons were given the special privilege of access to a room near the archives and still depended on the archivist who alone could use the catalogues and enter the archive itself.

Meanwhile the intention to make access easier – we must not yet think of an intention to make access easy – caused the making of a room for students. The Pope allocated space for a new reading-room, on the ground floor of the long west side the Vatican palace. In the summer of 1880 the Pope visited the reconstruction to see progress. On 1 January 1881 it was officially opened, so that it was now physically possible for more students to use the archives. This was an enormous improvement, welcomed gladly by everyone. But it was not yet comfortable. It was formerly a coach-house. Its outlook was east, the sun did not penetrate, the floor was stone, there was no heating, and the atmosphere was dank. Men afterwards looked back upon their endeavours in this room as years of physical suffering. In winter they sat there hat on head, huddled in cloaks, feet in a fur-lined warmer, and still chilled to the bone. Over the door of the archives was still inscribed the threat of excommunication. The staff was still tiny, wholly inadequate to the number of persons who now gained the privilege of access. Men could not see the catalogues, or go to the archives for themselves. They were still dependent on the archivists – which meant, Monsignor Balan. Balan was willing to communicate documents. But like his predecessors he insisted on the payment of proper fees; if a government mission were seeking copies of all letters concerning the history of their country, the copying could be a heavy expense. The Austrians solved it by persuading Balan to accept a lump sum for a year and then being allowed to get copies of as many documents as they needed. Those who worked much at the archives were conscious of a struggle behind the scenes; Hergenröther always working towards more freedom, but having little influence with the Curia, dependent on a good relationship with the Pope, and useful to the Pope because of his European reputation; Balan determined to keep access restricted and a privilege, and backed in this policy by the Secretary of State and a majority of the cardinals in the Curia. Balan could be helpful. He could be ice-cold to men whose enquiries he distrusted. Much seemed to hang on Hergenröther not dropping dead. He was delicate, and whenever his health drooped, anxiety swept over the workers in the archive that soon the doors would again be shut.[41] Some believed that the terrible discomfort of the archives in winter was caused by cardinals who disliked the Pope's policy. They could not reverse the Pope's decision, but could see that no one enjoyed its consequence.

In the spring of 1883 Sickel, head of the Austrian institute in Rome, achieved an important victory.[42]

One of the reasons for all this difficulty was a realistic doctrine about human nature. Men cannot help being what they are, and historians are also men. A historian educated as a Protestant, or professing a Protestant faith, may strive for impartiality. But he will never be able to see the history of the Catholic Church in an impartial light, because this is beyond the capacity of human nature into which bias is built by origin and parentage and education. Admit the most high-minded scholar among Protestants to the Secret Archives, and he cannot help but use his matter, in the end and however he conceal it, to attack the Catholic Church. This was the axiom of those who supported Balan and resisted the liberalizing policy of Hergenröther. Pope Leo XIII shared the belief. He had at first no intention of relinquishing strict control over access to the archives.

In April 1883 Theodor Sickel shook the doctrine. He had been working on the document known as the *Privilegium Ottonis* in which the German Emperor Otto the Great bestowed gifts upon the see of Rome. The document was often assailed as a papal forgery. Sickel, allowed since 1881 to work at the archives and to use the original, convinced himself that the document was authentic, and printed his conclusion to the world.

Here was a case of a Protestant demolishing anti-Catholic propaganda, directly because he was allowed access to the Vatican Secret Archives. Nothing could be more welcome to Cardinal Hergenröther as he sought to defend a liberal attitude against its numerous critics. The Pope did not read German. Hergenröther wrote for the Pope a special report on the contents of Sickel's book.

On 10 April 1883 the Pope gave Sickel a private audience, private except that Sickel's wife also came (Sickel had not expected her but she was determined not to miss the occasion). Sickel presented him with a copy of his book on the *Privilegium Ottonis*. The Pope took the book, and opened it, and then began to talk about its contents, and to say how welcome was the result. Then he said: 'But what will the German critics say about it?' He expressed a doubt whether historians in Protestant lands would ever be able to write about the Pope objectively. Sickel defended Protestant scholars warmly, his wife thought too warmly. The Pope seemed to think that because Sickel defended the *Privilegium Ottonis* as authentic, and saved the Church from the charge of forgery, he must have stopped being a Protestant. 'Because I agreed with him on the historical fact,' wrote Sickel afterwards, 'he was inclined to think that I must be denying my faith.'[43]

This friendly conversation was soon the subject of talk in the Vatican. Hergenröther perhaps spread the news. Sickel found that the iciness of Balan's manner disappeared. In the same month the Pope promoted Balan to be a referendary in the Signatura Justitiae – that is, the old high court before 1870 which since Italian occupation had no function, but which still carried a stipend. It would be too much to say that from Sickel's book the authorities gained a more favourable attitude to Protestant scholars in general. But they began to be more helpful to Sickel.

Sickel's work on Otto the Great was diversified by an extraordinary incident. When he first got into the archives, he asked to see the *Liber Diurnus*, which Acton had wanted to rescue from Rome during the turmoils of 1870. He asked Cardinal Hergenröther if he might see the manuscript. Hergenröther refused him all help – the territory was too delicate. As Sickel worked away at the manuscript of the *Privilegium Ottonis*, he asked if he might see other early manuscripts to compare the hand. The junior archivist Gregorio Palmieri brought him several manuscripts of a like date. Sickel at once recognized that one of them was the original manuscript of the *Liber Diurnus*. Palmieri had evidently no idea what he brought. Sickel said nothing at the time. A few days later he talked to Hergenröther of the possibility of a new edition. Hergenröther reacted strongly against. Sickel's edition of the *Liber Diurnus* appeared at last eight years later.

Lord Acton, fascinated as ever by the opening of archives, was struck by the effect of Sickel's work on the *Privilegium Ottonis*. Earlier in his life the discovery of archives seemed to be the demolition of pious legends and respectabilities, the uncovering of scandals which men tried to hide. 'What archives reveal,' he wrote in his private notes, 'is the wickedness of men.' 'The one constant result is to show that people are worse than their reputation.'[44] The archives now looked as though they could help to destroy, not merely an excess of credulity, but an excess of scepticism. Men denied that a document was authentic, and alleged it to be forged in the interests of an institution; and then scientific history came and showed that after all it was genuine. In one of his private notes now in the Cambridge University Library Acton wrote: 'Correct the excess of criticism by aid of Sickel, the prince of critics.'[45]

The next move in this history was primarily caused by a sudden and unpredictable intervention on the part of the aged Garibaldi.

On 31 March 1882 Palermo commemorated with processions, speeches and illuminations the medieval massacre known as the Sicilian Vespers. The French happened to be unpopular in Italy at that moment, because of their activities in Tunis, and the festival was at first suspected of being an anti-French demonstration, though Italian politicians took care to deny the charge. The procession was orderly, the celebration devout, the speeches glorified a united and free Italy, but were not anticlerical or antipapal, not even the speech at the church of the Martorana by Crispi who was deputy for Palermo and famous as an anticlerical. Garibaldi himself, old and dying, was not able to take part in the ceremonies and was represented by his son. But he sent a letter, in his most oratorical form. And by this letter an old Sicilian massacre became connected with the opening of the Vatican Secret Archives.

It was addressed: 'to Thee, Palermo, mistress of the art of expelling tyrants, belongs the sublime right of driving out of Italy the prop of all tyrannies – the corrupter of nations – who dwelling on the right bank of the Tiber, unleashes thence his black hounds for the destruction of universal suffrage – almost gained – after having tried to sell Italy for the hundredth time. Remember, O brave people, that from the Vatican blessings were sent to the mercenaries whom in 1282 thou didst drive away with such heroism...'[46]

Pope Leo XIII meditated long on this flourish by the old foe. The point was the belief that popes were enemies of Italy, Italian freedom, Italian prosperity. His idea of history included different evidence: how popes at the end of the Roman Empire helped to preserve Italy from barbarian invasion; popes in the Middle Ages defended Italy successfully against the power of German emperors; popes in the Counter-Reformation defended Italy from Turkish raids, and helped Austria to defend all Europe from Turkish conquest; even within the nineteenth century popes helped to save Italy from the domination of Napoleon Bonaparte. As he contemplated these historic examples, Leo saw the Papacy not as the enemy of Italian liberty, Italian culture or Italian nationality, but as their chief creator.[47]

Then how have Garibaldi and (the Pope confessed) so many others gained so erroneous an impression? Because history was corrupt. Not only Protestants but Italian Catholics treated history as a weapon of propaganda against the Church. 'They use Christian history in a powerful and clever way, especially when they treat the history of the Popes in its relation to the history of Italy...' They use old and long refuted legends, seize on whatever is ill in private life, omit all the grandeur of the past, make historical characters ridiculous, fail to base themselves on authentic documents. The lies creep into newspapers, the theatre, even textbooks in schools. 'Out of history they have brewed a poison', *venenum malum historia facere.* Today it can truly be said, *artem historicam coniurationem hominum videri adversus veritatem*, the historian's art looks like conspiracy against the truth.

So far then from the Church shunning the truth of history, we need more history; better history, less propagandist history, written by men looking for truth and not for weapons, history less superficial.

No pope since Benedict XIV, nearly a century and a half before, had held such view on the nature of historical enquiry, or even realized how powerfully history could act upon present opinion.

On 18 August 1883 Pope Leo XIII published a Letter to the Three Cardinals. The three were de Luca, the vice-chancellor whose office had by ritual tradition a historic connection with the library; Pitra, the Frenchman who was Cardinal-protector of the library but had no real power; and Hergenröther, who though prefect of the archives had real but not supreme power in the archives. The contents of the letter made it one of the most important utterances by a pope in modern times.

Here Leo XIII uttered all his fears at the corruption of history. We need true history, better history, impartial history. We need to show the Italian people what they owe to the popes of past centuries. Let men work at the sources; use prudence and not rashness in judgment; avoid the superficial. The first law of history is that *nothing untrue be said, and nothing true be unsaid.* It is a noble study. From the historian Eusebius onwards, the Church has ever encouraged history. In the Middle Ages the monasteries preserved the historical sense. In modern times Baronius and Muratori made great contributions, and although some things in Muratori were reprehensible no one did more for the history of Italy.

In this century came Angelo Mai. I have already opened the archives for 'religious and good' study and do the same now for the library. Would that many might undertake the study of history. For it all speaks loud to us of God, *clamat enim quodammodo omnis historia Deum esse.* History shows how Rome is rightly the seat of the Pope and the government of the Christian Church. The perfect philosophy of history was given to us by St Augustine. Those who have held to his ideas have studied rightly, those who have left him have gone astray.

Pope Leo XIII, those historians who knew him were agreed, had little interest in history and small sense of historical method. But he had a profound feeling for the harmony between Christianity and the best in European culture, and had the courage and integrity to apply this to history. He had the simple view that history, rightly understood, would prove even the temporal power of the popes to be necessary, and his commendation of St Augustine's philosophy of history was as unpalatable to some of the scientific historians as his commendation of St Thomas Aquinas was unpalatable to some philosophers.

Besides professing a love of historical truth, the Pope may have seen an advantage in history. Within Italy continued a mighty struggle of parties, between the liberal middle-classes who wanted a united Italy under the house of Savoy, and the peasants with devout members of the upper class who looked to the Pope and were not reconciled either to united Italy or to the house of Savoy. Who was the more authentic representative of historic Italy? – the Pope, or the King of Piedmont suddenly swollen to be king of all Italy? He who looked into history could not doubt the answer. The Pope was the ruler of a thousand years and more, the king from Savoy was a modern upstart. Within the strife of Italian parties, the argument from history was important to the Pope's servants.

The Pope himself never articulated publicly this usefulness of history for his party. But some of his servants – Balan among them – were fully aware of its importance. At the Catholic Congress at Modena, in October 1879, Balan made a speech which was reprinted in thirty editions, on the historic advantages which flowed from the Papacy to all Italy.[48]

But Leo's letter was far weightier than these points of controversy. It stood out, and caught the imagination of educated Europe, that this Pope had no fear of history. *The Church has no anxiety before the truth* – that was what men read from the reports in their newspapers.

The response to the Letter to the Three Cardinals was not uniformly friendly. Inside the Curia men instantly saw that the Pope effectively committed them to allowing all responsible persons to have free access to library and archives, and some of them were not pleased. Even the secretary of the Austrian embassy at the Vatican was not eager at the idea of more enquirers being let loose among the records – it might open the doors to more falsification of history and partisan writing.[49] A few Protestants ungenerously criticized the assumption in the letter that 'impartial' history would be sure to produce an ultramontane conclusion. But what struck the world was the appeal to history – that is, to impartial and critical enquiry – and the free declaration that the private records would be open to inspection. Soon afterwards (24 February 1884) Leo addressed a meeting of the Görres Society, the German Catholic Society for the study of history. He was blunt. 'Go to the sources. That is why I have opened the archives to you. We are not afraid of people publishing documents out of them', *non abbiamo paura della pubblicità dei documenti*.[50]

The Italian liberal newspapers treated the Letter to the Three Cardinals with respect, and at that date this was extraordinary. They contrasted this appeal to critical enquiry with an old spirit of excommunication. On 29 August 1883 the London *Times* wrote a leader upon the theme, and upon the contrast between Pope Pius IX and Leo XIII. Pope Pius could not publish an encyclical against corruption and sensuality, of which all men acknowledge the inroads, without making modern thought bristle with hostility. Pope Leo denounces all history but ultramontane history, from Ranke to Father Gavazzi, and the most uncompromising adversaries express their thanks. This was unjust of *The Times*, which in those years could be unjust on such themes. Its leading article was surprisingly scornful of the invitation to the archives. 'It is as if the Governor of the Bank of England were to stand in Threadneedle Street and request passers-by to help themselves from the cellars and tills.'

This leader of *The Times* was not so unfriendly as professionally anti-Catholic newspapers. The London *Record* wrote in its main leader (14 September 1883), 'Leo XIII, having discovered that history is a dangerous witness, proposes that this witness be tampered with.' In an article which contained two large historical errors, it urged its readers to encourage historical works of a sound Protestant tendency. Like Pope Pius IX, the *Record* did not suppose that the historian could peel off his bias. But the important thing was the extent of the European welcome, especially remarkable among the Italian liberal newspapers, several of which portrayed the Pope as abandoning the era of attack upon the modern world which was the era of Pope Pius IX, and turning to the era of enquiry and discussion.

The three cardinals, charged by the Pope's letter to engage in historical enquiries, became a commission for the purpose.

The work of this commission, and of the sub-commission which it appointed, are little known because it bore little fruit, and was regarded by the true workers in the archive with a measure of contempt. We have an account of the debates on the commission in the biography of one of its members, Cardinal Pitra.[51]

The cardinals began by contemplating a plan to publish everything, and out of the authentic documents create a true history of the Catholic Church. They soon realized two defects of the plan; first that it was impossible, and second that it was inexpedient. It was impossible because it was gigantic, would require vast sums of money which were unobtainable and very numerous workers, trained in research, who were not to be found, and would take a century or centuries to execute. It was inexpedient because it would become 'official history', history under the patronage of the Pope. As historians Pitra and Hergenröther were aware that history is never final and that error creeps in at every throw. If they created an official history, it would soon be despised under some such name as 'Manipulation of history for the use of popes'.

Some wanted to write the history of the first three centuries only; some to continue the Annals of Baronius into modern times; some wanted biographies of popes or ecclesiastics; they talked of a Church history for training the clergy, a popular Church history for the people. Cardinal Pitra put forward what he regarded, strangely, as a 'modest' plan, more manageable. There should be a two-volume 'centre of work', that is, a series of facts showing the see of Rome within the plans of providence; and then the inferences from these facts to establish and confirm the papal monarchy; and then to illustrate in far more detail, especially 'the epoch of the moral greatness of Italy, from the age of Leo X to the age of Pius IX and Leo XIII, with the popes profiting by the peace to show themselves magnificent in literature and art and architecture'. Pitra really wanted, what Pope Leo XIII himself seems to have expected, a history which would show historical inevitability in the Pope's power, temporal as well as spiritual, and lead to the climax of the first Vatican Council.

Something like this proposal of Pitra was formally adopted. A Capuchin friar, Father Marcellino da Civezza, who was already distinguished as the author of a history of Franciscan missions, was selected for the task of writing the book on the place of the pope in Italian history. He was not pleased at being given the task, but Pope Leo personally summoned him and laid upon him the burden. Even while he was writing three volumes in an unaccustomed field, he was pressed to make haste; and made haste to such purpose, that he had the three volumes ready for the printer within eighteen months. The circumstances did not make for an impartial tone, and the book was not well received.

The difficulties had only begun. The Pope sounded as though he expected historians to grow plentifully out of the ground. It was Pitra's duty to recruit foreign workers of good will; for this project would need not only the Vatican Archives but all the great archives of Europe. The Pope told Cardinal Manning, whose ideas of history were not quite his own, that he would call to Rome one or two experts from each country, and asked Manning to select and recommend names.[52] Pitra found that the men who were expert were already committed and could not give the time, while he suffered marvellous trials from amateurs who wanted the Pope to pay the expense of their research theses. One man offered them an outline history of the Papacy already in manuscript, another offered to sell them an anti-Jesuit history of the Jesuits, alleging its special value because the Jesuits had destroyed the only other two copies. Meanwhile the sub-commission in effect took over the cardinals' commission, and finally the indignant Pitra (16 May 1884) resigned; though, to avoid European scandal, he promised the Pope not to make the resignation public. The best thing, perhaps the only thing, which the cardinals' commission achieved was encouragement to the publication of papal registers. The Pope appointed Canon Isidoro Carini from Palermo as professor of palaeography in connection with the archives.

Carini, who had been archivist in the city of Palermo, came to the Pope's attention by publishing documents on the massacre of the Sicilian Vespers. The Vatican acquired five large new machines for all the printing it would need to do under the grand design.[53]

The men working in the archives took little notice of the cardinals' commission. They went their way, each intent on his plans; Augustin Sauer from Breslau commemorated the saving of Vienna from the Turks in 1683 by 200 documents from the Secret Archives; Father Pietro Pressutti, who once worked with Theiner, was engaged on Pope Honorius III; Father Calenzio was at work on the documents of Trent; Berger on Innocent IV; Hergenröther on Leo X; Sickel and his Austrian pupils on the medieval Empire; and Balan himself on Luther as seen through the documents in the archives. What interested the men working was not the plan or plans of the cardinals' commission, but the struggle which still continued within the archives, between Cardinal Hergenröther who was prefect without much power and wished to open, and his sub-archivist Balan who had nearly all power and wished to keep tight control. Once this struggle took a physical, even a symbolic form. Hergenröther came into the archives soon after seeing the Pope and finding him delighted that a Protestant like Sickel could reach such un-Protestant conclusions over the *Privilegium Ottonis*. Hergenröther saw Sickel working there, and taking no notice of the Catholics saluting him with the customary genuflection, went straight to Sickel to greet him, took him by the arm, and started to lead him into the archive itself; through the door over which the inscription still threatened excommunication. Monsignor Balan leapt forward, seized Sickel by the coat tails, and dragged him back lest he be excommunicated. Hergenröther then showed Balan a paper with the Pope's special leave. Balan said that no one must know of the exception, and Sickel must not go through the door when others at the archive could see. So Sickel was taken the long way round through the door which led to the archives from the Sixtine library and which Pius IX once walled up.[54]

On 19 September 1883 Balan, who only five months earlier received titular promotion after promotion, was removed from all his offices. Gossip reported that he arrived at the archives to find that all the locks were changed and he could not get inside. The public reason given was ill-health. Few believed the story. The newspapers printed rumours over fees, even of selling documents; or that he wrote an anonymous pamphlet against the Pope's policy; or that in this age of conciliation his work on Luther was regarded as untimely; or that he had the intention of rewriting the history of Pope Clement XIV; or that he handed over to the Jesuits papers to their discredit from the time of Clement XIV; or that volumes vanished from the archives; or that he disagreed with the policy of opening the archives. To the newspaper *Euganeo* of Padua, one of the worst offenders, Monsignor Balan wrote a quiet letter denying the rumours. He said that Rome was bad for his health and therefore he went to North Italy. He publicly made his own the doctrine that *The Catholic Church and the Holy See have nothing to fear from the truth of history.* Retiring to the north, he continued his polemical history of Italy, eminent on the right wing of Italian politics.[55]

Balan was succeeded by Tosti, the monk of Monte Cassino already important to the grand design of publishing a universal history.[56] He was now called Vice-archivist. The scholars lamented his antiquity and respected his scholarship. Under him came Father Denifle from the Tyrol.

Documents of any year until 1815 were opened to scholars. The officials still had the right and duty to see and approve all copies or extracts. They had to decide whether the publication of a document, even before 1815, was contrary to a just regard for 'religious and social interests'. At first this disgusted some of the workers who regarded it as censorship. But throughout Hergenröther's reign the officers made less and less use of this right of inspection. The days when the archives were open increased. The time it took to get permission to work there fell from eight days or more to three or even two.

Formally the scholars were still not allowed to see the

catalogues. In fact the archivists allowed them an ever more frequent access to the catalogues. This was mainly due to Pietro Wenzel. While Hergenröther, and Balan, and Denifle continued their academic work and won European reputations, Wenzel had no desire for original work which lay so temptingly at every hand. He wanted only to establish order in the archives. While access was so restricted, the administration felt no special need to keep the catalogues in good order, and this was the reason why some documents were still hard to find. Because the archive was composed of a collection of archives, it had an ill-ordered collection of catalogues. Part of the reason for refusing access to catalogues was shame. Pietro Wenzel started collecting, grouping, ordering the various catalogues and indices, and brought them together in one place. The rule – no access – remained in force, and was partly obeyed. It was fully obeyed only with newcomers, or at moments of crisis, as when a Prussian historian launched an improper attack upon the Vatican Secret Archives at a German historical congress in Nuremberg.[57]

Wenzel's care became important in other ways. The rules became hard to keep because the enquirers were too many for the staff. Leo XIII intended to provide more staff, but money was short, and the customers grew far more rapidly than perhaps he expected. Since Heinrich Denifle had a scholarly place apart, the burden of coping with seventy or more scholars fell heavily upon the shoulders of Wenzel. Without his laborious work the archive would hardly have remained a workable institution. Naturally he could only carry the burden by sometimes taking short cuts. And from his youthful behaviour towards Joseph Stevenson, we know that Wenzel thought rules to be made for historians, not historians for rules.

Legends went about Europe that this opening was all show. Hostile ignoramuses believed that the Pope pretended to open his archive but kept back anything discreditable. This legend was nourished by the early cases where Hergenröther still refused to allow enquirers to see what they wanted – denying

Sickel access at first to the *Liber Diurnus,* or refusing to let Franz Xaver Kraus see papers of Pope Benedict XIV.[58] But anyone who worked at length in the archives knew this alleged feat of selection to be impossible. To keep back what might hurt could only be done if the archivists knew the papers. The archivists had hardly more idea about the contents of the archives than the historians. They were themselves learning fast as applicants asked to see papers. The archivists must hand out to the student a large bundle of paper, docketed by subject, in complete ignorance of the separate letters in the bundle. Particular subjects might still be reserved, and a few special documents known to the archivists or the Pope. But the legend of systematic concealment postulated a system which did not exist. Sometimes a worker like Sickel knew more about the contents of an armarium than Wenzel or Denifle. When one student asked Wenzel for advice on how to proceed, he received the smiling reply *Bisogna pescare* – you have to go fishing.[59] This was and is the pain and pleasure of any worker in any archive – days of patience, hours of frustration, sudden excitement at a catch. In the Vatican of the eighteen-eighties the difficulty over the catalogues made the catches feel especially exciting and the times of patience especially frustrating.

But now came a big test; a test of the policy-makers, whether they believed in their own policy of freedom, and a test of the policy, whether it could fulfil the expectations of those responsible: the argument over the papers of the worst of all popes (meaning by 'worst' nothing to do with ability for he was also one of the ablest) Alexander VI Borgia. For a moment in this debate the new policy came near to shipwreck.

6

The Borgia Pope

Catholic historians had not tried to paint the Borgia Pope white. In the official continuation of the Annals of Baronius Rinaldi uttered a condemnation. Catholic historians of the nineteenth century, like Möhler and Hergenröther, were frank. Before he became a cardinal, in his handbook of Church history, Hergenröther wrote: 'As Cardinal, Borgia was immoral and vicious. As Pope he was unworthy, and at his death Christendom was delivered from a great scandal.'[1] When Catholics were open, anti-Catholic historians like Gregorovius helped themselves to the evidence and anti-Catholic journalists like Victor Hugo helped themselves to more than the evidence.

The argument over papal power in the middle of the nineteenth century drew the attention of the world to bad popes. In theory the authority of the institution in matters of faith was nothing to do with the morality of the occupants of the office. But it seemed to have much to do, and bad popes, or whether popes were bad, were parts of the European debate. Inevitably at such a season the apologists intruded. In the very year of the Vatican Council a Dominican defended Pope Alexander VI as maligned. In the year that Pius IX died a German published an apologia at Regensburg. Two years later an Italian produced at Bologna three volumes of whitewash.[2] The debate took a European form. Even while Lord Acton was intent upon the business of the Vatican Council, he found time to write for the *North British Review* a learned and balanced article on 'The Borgias and their latest historian'.[3]

Lady Paget, wife of the British ambassador to the government of Italy, recorded an enchanting picture from that socially awkward age. As her husband was accredited to the Italian government which the Curia regarded as invaders, she was not welcome in the company of cardinals. Whether in error or not, she and her daughter were invited to a party at the Corsini Palace, and found themselves among all the 'black' society of clerical Rome, with a kind of altar raised on a dais against the wall. She sensed consternation at her coming. Then seminarists began to repeat poetry in praise of past popes; until a nine-year-old, with a high treble voice, recited verses in honour of 'our good pope Alexander VI' and followed with a panegyric on the Borgias. This was too much for the young Miss Paget, who disgraced the family and Britain by mirth.[4]

The new rules of the archives decreed that though the papers were normally available till 1815, 'for religious and social interests' the officials might refuse access to documents of a date before that year.

When Theiner ruled the archives, an Austrian scholar asked to see Burchard's diary, which he believed to contain lurid passages on the Borgia Pope. He reported to a friend that the diary was kept under lock and key like some demon which it was dangerous to let loose.[5] Theiner himself looked at Burchard's diary, and thought the contents not so awful. 'Borgia,' Theiner said to a German friend, 'was not such a monster, and the contents of the Diary are not so romantic, as people think.'[6] But when no one but Theiner knew what was in the original, it was better to keep away prying eyes.

Yet, when the subject was argued in European journals, and the archives were opening in other directions, it was neither easy nor wise to maintain silence. In 1881 one of Theiner's French friends found that two whitewashers denied the authenticity of a famous letter about the early life of Cardinal Borgia. He applied to the archives, and asked Cardinal Hergenröther and Monsignor Balan whether the original existed. Balan freely replied that it did; and more, he carefully collated the manuscript with the printed text to report variations.[7] Yet the men working inside the archives, like the Austrian scholars, knew this area to be prohibited. They heard that Pope Leo XIII particularly wished no one to pursue research upon that Pope.

Late in November 1885 the leader of the Hungarian scholars in Rome, Fraknói,[8] went to dinner with some cardinals and lamented that the papal registers were still scattered in various places and therefore it was impossible to work on them as a collection. He had it specially at heart that some registers lay not in the Vatican Archives but in the Lateran Palace – including those of Leo X on which Cardinal Hergenröther was working. These were the archives of the Datary which suffered such losses when Napoleon stole the papers. Among the cardinals present was Cardinal Sacconi, lately become dean of the Sacred College, and as Prodatary the responsible guardian of the Lateran Archives. Sacconi was rightly believed to have opposed Leo XIII at the papal election, and known to be against the policy of opening the archives. The Hungarians were therefore surprised when Sacconi offered to let Fraknói into the Lateran Archive. Since the Hungarians worked closely with the Austrians, Fraknói got leave also for Sickel, and for their assistants.

The nominal archivist at the Lateran was a lawyer, aged 73 and too gout-ridden to work. He left affairs, in traditional manner, to the hands of his young nephew. For the proper fee it was agreed that the nephew should open the Lateran Archive to these Austro-Hungarians and shut it again in the evening. As the nephew had never before entered the archive, he could not be expected to give much help. He was supposed to guard over them, but sensibly removed himself for meals and left them to their picnics.

They (that is, two Hungarians, eight Austrians and a German visitor, eleven in all) found themselves in a big room with shelves reaching to the ceiling about twenty feet high, folios on all the shelves, top shelves so high that they could not read the titles on the spines of the top books even with the aid of opera glasses. They reckoned there to be some 3,000 folio volumes. The old archivist had told them that there was no catalogue. They needed ladders, and found none. The volumes of Leo X stood on one side for Hergenröther's use. On the lower shelves the registers stood arranged in order of popes and chronologically by years; but they soon saw that the arrangement was disorderly. Under Pius II they found volumes of Pius V, under Pius IV volumes of Pius II. The room contained no tables nor chairs on which they could put books or work. They had to lay volumes all over the floor. But the floor was covered with the dust of years. They offered the nephew money to get cleaning equipment from the custodians of the palace, but for all their papers of licence from Cardinal Sacconi the custodians were suspicious, did not know the nephew, and would not help. They took off their overcoats and jackets and laid them on the floor. The more agile of the party climbed up the shelves and got a few volumes off the top registers. A couple of shaky ladders were found. By the next day they thought they had enough to survey a whole pontificate, and the nephew produced benches and tables. They worked away finding documents about Austrian monasteries or Hungarian churches. But it was exhausting, and after an hour they started climbing again and arranging more volumes.

At this point they noticed that they were fetching down volumes of the register of Pope Alexander VI Borgia. And they knew already, even if Cardinal Sacconi had not mentioned it, that Pope Leo XIII would not approve. The discovery brought them up with a jolt. They carefully put back the folios.[9]

They worked there for most of four days, and made no concealment of what they did when they met the archivists at the Vatican Secret Archives. They said frankly that many of the volumes were in disarray and they were trying to put them back in better order. On 26 November one of the archivists, Gregorio Palmieri, came round at their invitation to see what they were doing.

Palmieri had never before entered the Lateran Archive. He saw hundreds of volumes higgledy-piggledy (so it looked) on a dusty floor. Sickel did not like to think what he said in his report to Cardinal Hergenröther. Whatever he said, it must have been lurid, for the response was swift. That same evening the Lateran archivist received a special order from the Pope quashing the permission given by Cardinal Sacconi. He sent out his nephew, who sought Sacconi and failed to find him; then sought Fraknói and failed to find him; and so came to Sickel. Sickel was not surprised. He was conscious of an atmosphere of mounting tension through the week. Sacconi had allowed them to break all the rules – to go into an archive itself, to use an archive not properly in order, to handle the volumes as though they were themselves the archivists, and all without proper supervision. They had also been allowed to take off the shelves the registers of Pope Alexander VI Borgia, about whom Pope Leo XIII had a special feeling for confidentiality;[10] and even though they behaved with perfect honour, that was not known to the Pope and perhaps was even irrelevant. The Pope demanded the keys of the Lateran Archive and put sentries on the door. He refused entry even to the archivist, even to Cardinal Hergenröther.

Cardinal Sacconi had not been consulted and was offended at this invasion of his duties. The Austro-Hungarians heard the story that he said he would not put up with it even from a Pope.[11] The argument developed into a battle over jurisdiction within the Curia. Hergenröther saw all his liberal plans endangered by these foreign busybodies, and at first would listen to no excuses. The atmosphere at the archives became cold as never since the days of Monsignor Rosi-Bernardini. The Austrian ambassador had to intercede for his nationals. Sickel felt a strong desire to keep a low profile. 'We did not mean to raise the dust, but we have, and must now be as quiet as we can.' It was even rumoured that at the Lateran they built for themselves a table out of folio volumes.

The 'invasion' of the Lateran, as it was described in a hostile newspaper, gave a chance to those who disliked Leo XIII's policy about the archives. The opponents now consisted of three different groups, with diverse aims. Old-fashioned opponents like Cardinal Bianchi simply thought it wrong to open documents to uncontrollable enquiry. But some who had not wished to open, were now dead or converted. Secondly, a group of Italian scholars, using Tosti as their figurehead, regarded the contents of the archive as part of the history of the Italian nation, in which Italian historians should rightly be granted a privileged place; and freely criticized the liberal policy that these archives were open to any reputable person, whatever his nationality or his religion. That Sickel was neither a Catholic nor an Italian became for a moment a weighty argument. Thirdly, a few serious and informed men saw risks in the discrepancy between many students and few archivists, recognized the danger of damage to documents or even loss, and knew that the archive was only just workable and but for Pietro Wenzel could easily be unworkable. Some learned men certainly took home documents from the archives that they might more easily copy them in the evenings,[12] and this was a way to risk loss. The invasion of the Lateran, a glaring instance of unsupervised students, gave occasion to these varied critics of Leo's policy.

The Pope held on his way. A week later all was over. On 28 November Cardinal Sacconi proposed to the Pope that the relevant volumes of Lateran registers be loaned to the Vatican Archives. Hergenröther agreed next day. Pope Leo XIII ordered the temporary transfer from Lateran to Vatican of the 400-odd volumes of registers which the Austro-Hungarians needed for their work. Denifle and the Vatican archivists could not at first believe in the order. They were probably pleased at the outcome, for the volumes never returned to the Lateran. Later all the other registers followed them. These registers nominally belonged to the Datary. In 1892 all the papers of the Datary were transferred to the Vatican.

Afterwards a few German professors were inclined to pooh-pooh Sickel's work. They were wrong. This lively and choleric man, with plump figure, greying beard, and full red face, looking more like a farmer than a scholar, led the European field in developing the knowledge of medieval handwriting and the nature of medieval official documents. Though he never ceased to be a north German by origin and a Protestant, he became important to Leo XIII as a man who by his impartiality vindicated the decision that the archives should be open. Almost as soon as the Pope opened the archives, Sickel realized that the new opportunity needed more than individuals working independently, it required an institute organized with the intention of getting what could be got from the Vatican Archives. The Austrian Institute was first formed (1883) with the personal backing of the Emperor Francis Joseph. In 1890–3 it won the public and financial support of the Austrian government. During those first seven years after the foundation Sickel needed to convince sceptics in Vienna that what he planned could be done and that the Vatican Archive would not soon be closed. Within the archive his never-ending demands, and his knowledge not only of the manuscripts but of their armaria or cupboards, showed Wenzel and Denifle what must be done to get the archive into better order. When Sickel started, he could hardly see an index. When Sickel left Rome in 1901, Wenzel had collected all the indexes into a single place of consultation.

Three months after the escapade at the Lateran Palace, Ludwig Pastor finished the printing of volume 1 of the *History of the Popes.*

Ludwig Pastor was born at Aachen on 31 January 1854, with a Protestant father and Catholic mother. His father died when the child was young. When he was six the family moved to Frankfurt, and the boy was sent to the 'Simultan-gymnasium' of the city, providing education for both Catholics and Protestants.

Here he met the extraordinary man among the Catholic historians of Germany. Johannes Janssen had the duty of teaching history to the Catholic boys in the school. He had not yet designed the monumental history which was intended to shatter the Protestant historians' account of the German Reformation. But he was already publishing solid work. Himself a dedicated student and a Catholic so unyielding as to be always controversial, he communicated to the young Pastor the passion for historical study and simultaneously the belief that Protestant professors portrayed the Catholic past in a partisan light and must be countered. This great-German Catholicism was strengthened in Pastor because the formative years as he left school were the years of Bismarck's struggle with the Catholic Church. The Catholic historian began by seeing as his vocation the defence of Catholicism; which is not to say that he did not also see his vocation as the duty to write true history.

Janssen gave him to read *The History of the Popes* by Leopold von Ranke. Ranke's history was written early in his life, during the eighteen-thirties (first edition 1834–9). Remote from polemical interests, it took the history of popes for the first time out of the controversies inherited from the Reformation. It made Ranke's European reputation as an objective historian, and went through edition after edition (seventh edition in 1878). It was one important sign of the new flowering of European historical writing, and the new kind of historical writing, during the second quarter of the nineteenth century.

But a historian can never escape altogether from himself. For all his Olympian detachment Ranke was a devout Lutheran. Something about the attitude, atmosphere, even selection of documents, did not please the Catholic reader of an ultramontane age in the nineteenth century. Janssen said of Ranke that he made little popes great and great popes little – and nevertheless his work was the best he had written. And it stopped at the beginning of the nineteenth century, when the papacy was fallen to its lowest. Janssen handed the book to Pastor with a purpose. On 8 December 1873 Pastor had a kind of religious experience. 'It was as if a higher power said to me: *Take your pen and write a Catholic history of the popes of that age.*'

The original idea, then, was anti-Ranke history. It was also *a Catholic history*: written by a Catholic without the hostile eyes of Protestant historians. Pastor wrote about Ranke, 'You cannot describe the reality of the fifteenth and sixteenth century with gloves made of ice.'[13]

Meanwhile he was not ripe for any undertaking of the kind. He wandered through the universities of Louvain, Bonn, Berlin and Vienna. Among the historians of Vienna he found his second master, Onno Klopp. Klopp was another convert to Roman Catholicism. As a Protestant he was the archivist of the kingdom of Hanover, and when Prussia swallowed Hanover in 1866, he went into exile at Vienna. Hating Prussia and Bismarck he became a Catholic in 1873 just when Bismarck's persecution of Roman Catholics reached its climax. Strong emotions spilled over into his historical studies. He gave Johannes Janssen quick impulse towards the anti-Lutheran cast of his history of the German Reformation. He called Leopold von Ranke, who by now was almost canonized in German historical study, 'the most dangerous of all Prussian liars'.[14]

But Pastor afterwards looked back upon this new mentor with gratitude for the opposite gift. He began with the idea that what the time needed was a Catholic historian who would smash Protestant history – that is, he had very old-fashioned ideas of his future task. Klopp brought him up with a jerk, that he was going wrong to his work. From Vienna in June 1877 he wrote to Klopp that although he knew how dangerous it was for a young unknown to make a frontal attack on Ranke, the leader of German history, or to attempt to show up Ranke as tendentious, 'I am not lacking in will or courage to grapple with Ranke.' He thought that he could start already with articles, and asked Klopp to help him out 'with a few pointers', and show the places where Ranke could be attacked.

Klopp to Pastor, 16 June 1877:

... It is not at all my opinion to encourage you to begin by attacking Ranke... Positive construction is far better than polemic. The objects of your polemic will not be convinced, they cannot be converted. We work for people who want to learn. They do not care whether some Berlin Professor has made a mistake or told a lie. They only care that they should be told what is true... I don't want you to write against him directly. I don't want you to write an Anti-Ranke. You would give his disciples the excuse to demolish you so far as they can. I stand on this point only; if on mature grounds you think a book is needed, don't be deterred from writing it by any consideration (whether favourable or unfavourable) for a person.

As he looked back later in life, Pastor felt that he owed to Klopp the lesson that history is not polemic; and, slowly, that this is near to the axiom that history must not be apologetic and that the historian ceases to be a historian in the moment that he becomes a conscious apologist for a cause.

Beginning at last his adult work, with a doctorate in front of his name, he decided to spend the winter of 1878–9 among the archives of Rome. He heard that recommendations were useless, and someone told him that if you saw documents at all, you saw them only through a grille.

The most important of the Roman archives is the Vatican Archive. It is my dearest wish to gain access to it. How difficult it is to break through the ban against using it, I heard from all sides when I was last in Rome.[15]

He started to get recommendations: his master Janssen, who was high in reputation at Rome – the rector of the German College in Rome de Waal – the papal nuncio in Munich – the papal nuncio in Vienna – the professor of Church history at Bonn – Monsignor de Montel, an Austrian prelate in Rome whom the Pope ordered to look after the dead Theiner's papers – Cardinal Pitra – and so up to Cardinal Nina the Secretary of State. Pastor arrived in Rome on 10 January 1879, to find that his difficulties were only beginning. On 13 January he applied to Cardinal Nina for access to the letters and reports of nuncios in Germany and France between 1542 and 1572 – with the particular object of refuting Ranke's *History of the Popes* in a Catholic spirit. Four days later Cardinal Nina gave him leave. But then Pastor found himself confronted by Monsignor Rosi the prefect, whose scruples cost ten days more. He wrote a fierce letter to Johannes Janssen against these obstructions. Janssen told him 'Don't be so hard on Rome. You are a newcomer and an unknown.'[16]

Pastor's diary is a fundamental source for the opening of

the Vatican Archives. But before I use it, I must pay attention
to its nature.

Pastor died at Innsbruck in 1928. In his last years, he used
the help of other scholars to finish his plan. One of these
assistants, Wühr, undertook the editing of the diaries and
letters, and, with the aid of Pastor's son in deciphering a
difficult hand, published in 1950 a fascinating volume, made
up out of extracts from diaries and letters. The papers, or most
of them, were then deposited by the widow in the Vatican
Library. For a time they were kept in the 'cupboard of honour'
which stands in the Vatican museum and contains Pastor's bust
and medals and printed works. Then the unprinted materials
were moved back to the Vatican Library.

This made possible a comparison between the original
diaries and Wühr's printed text of the diaries. The comparison
leaves a sense of mystery. The diaries of Wühr are not at all
the original diaries. The diaries of Wühr are a narrative,
composed as a diary, with the aid of the original diaries.
Presumably they were so composed not by Wühr but by Pastor,
even though Wühr mentioned in his preface that he filled out
some of Pastor's laconic utterances. What we are given in the
printed text looks like a contemporary comment of 1878. But
sometimes it is a reminiscence, perhaps composed in the
nineteen-twenties, and made up by putting down what
memory could bring to life by looking at the original text.

For example: the ecstatic moment in this history was the day
when Pastor first gained access to the archives, 27 January
1879. In the printed diary he described his feelings.

Today came the longed-for hour. To my great joy I could work for
the first time at the documents of the Vatican Secret Archives. At that
door of the archives which leads to the big room of the library I was
handed the first documents. They were the reports of the nuncio G.
Verallo from Germany...The extraordinary nature of the permission was in the complete use of the documents from a whole
pontificate (i.e. Paul III)...Added to that, the important privilege
of looking at the catalogue.

All this sounds like an entry written down that day, and the best of witness to his feelings. But the original diary is different. It says simply:

> 8–10   Vat. Bibl.
> 10¼   Vatik. Archiv
> Rel. di Verallo 1541–7

The words *Vatik. Archiv* were later underlined in blue.

This comparison between the full nature of the printed diaries and the laconic nature of the original diaries could be illustrated *ad infinitum*. We are not therefore to think that anything in the printed diaries is untrue. Nevertheless we must use the printed diaries with this amount of caution. Often they are autobiography, not diary; sometimes the autobiography of a man getting on in years. Therefore they are not to be quite trusted, especially about feelings and attitudes. He was seeing his entry to the archive, not as it felt that first day, but as it looked after thirty years of a fruitful life. Nor may we trust quite all the information. The first audience with Pope Leo XIII must have been unforgettable. But the papers show that he had the wrong date. The printed diary places it on 11 February 1879. The manuscript shows that it happened on 10 February 1879. The printed diary carries a whole description of the occasion lacking from the manuscript. That is natural. What is less natural is that the printed version altered the words of the Pope. Leo XIII told Pastor, 'Work *con amore* on the Popes and the Church and Religion.' For *work* Leo used the archaic word *travagliate*. In print Pastor altered the word to *lavorate*.

But the printed diary is still more mysterious. The jottings of the manuscript diary are not easy to read – Pastor's hand was small, script old-fashioned, abbreviations for his private eye. Whoever converted the entries of the manuscript diary into the printed diary could not always read the letters of the original. Sometimes he guessed, or altered the end of an illegible sentence to make at least sense. Perhaps the old man could not read his own youthful hand. But perhaps Wühr, who certainly wrought marvels with the handwriting, sometimes did the best he could with what he found; and if that happened, the printed diary might owe some sentences, not to Pastor at all, but to an endeavour to interpret him after he died.

All this is not to say that the printed diary does not bear a close relation to the manuscript diary. What is important is that the words of the printed diary are not always so contemporary as they seem, and thus far must be used with prudence by the historian.

In the winter of 1882–3, the winter after his marriage to the daughter of the mayor of Bonn, when he still had found no university to employ so papalist a writer, Pastor meditated again on Ranke. 'The Catholic historian must not be an apologist. This is a danger which presses in these controversial days. A historian who struggles for impartiality will not be so respected in his own day as the historian who is an apologist, for the second is the man of the moment. Later it is the other way round. The impartial historian does not die with his generation. The apologist is understood by his party, but to posterity is nothing but a pamphleteer. The historian must be free of political passion. A work of Catholic history ought to be like a splendid Romanesque cathedral, where the form eschews all ornament, and where the proportions are so perfect that the whole needs no embellishment.'[17]

At first his performance did not match his theory. From the earliest page of Edward Gibbon the reader knows himself in the hands of a master. This is not so with Pastor. The first edition of the first volume is the worst of the volumes. Pastor started to write while he still developed in technique, viewpoint and knowledge. The volume, published during 1886, was heavy with quotations. The language was still too strong – Valla's venom and virulence, 'overweening self-esteem' was a characteristic of all these critics of the Papacy in the age of the Renaissance. No one who read the first volume alone could have predicted what was to follow. It was not surprising that the candidature for professorships at Prague and Vienna failed. The volume won him a non-established ('extraordinary') professorship at Innsbruck in 1886, an established professorship in the following year.

Many of the reviewers were not unfriendly. The leaders of the German historical school smiled patronizingly at the papalism of the author but respected his learning and his archival enquiries. But from one quarter he had the hardest knock ever suffered by a historian of such future quality. In the learned journal of the University of Göttingen, another pupil of Döllinger, von Druffel, wrote a review intended to destroy Pastor for ever as a historian. The book, wrote Druffel, is nothing but a compilation; some of its passages are drawn nearly verbatim from other authors without acknowledgement; its archival researches are made to look impressive but are shoddy and superficial, two-thirds of the book is copied from elsewhere, it is thrown together in extraordinary carelessness – with chapter and verse cited at length for these vituperations.

More important for Pastor's future was the pleasure of Pope Leo XIII. In this first volume the Pope could read what he needed to hear. Leo XIII opened the Vatican Archives because Garibaldi and Italian anticlericals blamed popes for the ills of Italian history, and he had faith that authentic and impartial history would show the Papacy as a focus and strength of the best in Italian culture and Italian liberty. Pastor's first volume showed the Papacy at the heart of the Italian Renaissance. When the Pope read the book, and found its learning approved by reputable authors, he sent Pastor a brief, which Pastor placed in front of all future editions of his history. 'You could not use your talents more usefully, or more devoutly, than in describing with care and with truth, what was done by popes, who have suffered in repute by lapse of time or man's abuse.'[18]

Partly because of Druffel, but much more because of the contents of volume 1 and volume 2, Pastor did not win the serious attention of Protestant historians until his third volume. Despite Pastor's private ideals, the Protestants continued to regard him more as an apologist for popes than as an impartial historian, though they confessed that he was rare in his learning. Their attitude, if not justified, was in part excused by a certain quality in Pastor. His reputation as a papalist historian made it hard to find work – impossible to find a professorship in his German homeland. The only university which kept offering him a post was the Catholic University of Washington, and nowhere could be further from the archives which he needed. This refusal of German universities to take him seriously was excellent for the University of Innsbruck. But it had a consequence for his historical work. Geographically Innsbruck lay near the South German universities. But psychologically there was a gap. Pastor always remained outside the developing German school of Catholic history. All his life he was the lone writer unable to benefit much from exchange of views. His master Janssen was isolated from the movement of German scholarship which led the historical research of the world. Pastor was 'Janssen's man', sometimes called such by his critics, confessed as such by himself. He inherited Janssen's isolation, and never lost it to the end of his life.

He learnt to be a historian in the days when Prussia persecuted the Catholic Church, and the experience always marked him. German Catholic history learnt to make peace with a newer Germany and to feel less need to defend. But the German Catholic historians left Pastor behind, away across the mountain barrier. To the end of his life he was a man who lived through the fight with Bismarck, and for all his ideals could never shed from his history the strand of apology. The Catholics at the University of Freiburg-im-Breisgau refused to have him as a professor because he reminded them of an embattled age in the recent past which they preferred to forget. One critic accused him of not realizing until his dying day that Bismarck had ceased to attack the Catholic Church.

He had little sense of 'development', the key word in German historical minds. The Church was given, its hierarchy ordered. The quality which stands out in Pastor's Papacy is the unchanging quality of the institution. His piety, and a certain simplicity or even naiveté in his psychology, made it hard for him to see the point of view of those whose opinions he could not share. In this sense German Protestants were at first right in dismissing his history as apologia.

But their half-contempt changed suddenly with the publication of volume 3 in 1895. He had to come to Alexander VI Borgia. How would this alleged apologist cope? On 24 April 1888 he got the special leave necessary to see the documents, and worked at them by himself in Cardinal Hergenröther's room. He finished the draft of Alexander VI on 17 June 1892, and wrote in his diary, 'one of the saddest tasks that a Catholic historian has to do'.

The volume was excellently done; neither concealing anything, nor isolating and exaggerating the importance of the condemnations which he pronounced. This was a bigger historian than the author of the first volume. *He grows as he goes,* wrote the Jesuit reviewer in *Civiltà Cattolica.* It is highly to his honour, wrote the Protestant reviewer in the *English Historical Review.* 'Either he has trained himself by a special effort to discharge a specially difficult obligation, or, working as he had been for some years with the eye of historical criticism upon him, he has insensibly imbibed a more liberal sympathy and a more scientific method than seemed altogether assured by his first volume.'[19]

The Protestant critics still regretted what they called Pastor's 'dogmatism'. Richard Garnett wrote that when he read Bishop Creighton on the same subject he could not tell whether he was reading an ecclesiastic, whereas when he read Pastor (who was a layman) he was sure that he was reading an ecclesiastic. German universities continued to thwart all attempts to get Pastor a professorship in Germany. Despite these hesitations, public attitudes towards Pastor changed. The review which Pastor regarded as the most brilliant which his book ever received from any critic, Catholic or non-Catholic, was written by a Protestant.[20] He had an enormous power of work, was master of the literature, and supplied a mass of new documents henceforth indispensable to the enquirer. His new material was so far-ranging that he had the honour of being falsely accused, by good German historians, that he was not a man but a committee. Above all, he tried to tell the truth as he found it in the documents.

Then, should he have told? Was it right that a man who was regarded as an official historian of the popes should make such judgments, familiar in the mouths of Protestants? Was it right that such confessions should appear in a volume with a papal brief at its frontispiece? In June 1897 a Frankfurt friend, travelling from Rome through Innsbruck, told him that some of the Roman authorities were aggrieved about his book on Alexander VI Borgia. The friend also reported that Protestants in Rome had said to him 'Pastor cannot in his heart believe in the Papacy because he has found out so many of its weaknesses.'

Pastor said: 'Just because of the human weaknesses, which could not abolish Church and Papacy, I say the Church must be divine. Thank God, my historical studies have never caused the least qualm to my faith.'[21]

A lot of monsignori were still discontented. Even a cardinal or two thought that he ought not to have written. Cardinal Boggiani (a Dominican, whose order had just cause for doubting Pastor's story of their own Savonarola) believed that Pastor's History should be on the Index of Prohibited Books. Cardinal de Lai, grey eminence in the reign of Pope Pius X, told one of the papal chamberlains that he could not forgive Pastor for what he wrote about Pope Alexander VI. 'First charity and then truth,' said the cardinal, 'even in writing history'; *prima la carità e poi la verità anche nella storia.* Pastor heard the tale of what de Lai had said. 'If that were true,' he wrote, 'all history would be impossible. But Christ said, I am the truth.' The opposition in the Curia to Pastor's third volume could be detected even a quarter of a century later. It was always a small group, because Pope Leo XIII recommended volume 3 equally with the others. So far as present evidence goes, Pope Leo wavered not an instant in his support for Pastor.

Though Pastor could get no professorship in Germany (except an offer from Münster which had too small a library for his purposes), he was at last rewarded in 1901, when he succeeded the Protestant Sickel as head of the Austrian Institute in Rome. Even then, Vienna told him, 'You get the job in spite of, and not because of, your religious attitude. You have deserved it by your History.'[22]

The work was done. The Vatican Secret Archives were open to the historian. Pope Leo XIII did something which no one could undo. The rest was tidying.

Hergenröther planned a better room for students, a long white room, on a level with the street, with high wide windows overlooking the street, and a wooden floor instead of the dank stone, but still with no heating because men were afraid of fire, still with nowhere to hang wet mackintoshes on rainy days, and outside the clatter of horses' hooves as tourists drove up to the museums. The cardinal just failed to live long enough to see this room opened, for he died on 3 October 1890. His death caused anxiety.

For nearly forty years the historians did not lose their nervousness that someone, librarian or archivist or prefect or pope, would again shut what was open. The archive was accessible because Pope Leo XIII had faith in truth and because he trusted his new prefect of the archives, Cardinal Hergenröther. Towards the end of the century, when the Cardinal-archivist was a famous diplomat and knew nothing of archives, men said that the Cardinal-archivist was a mere titular office.[23] This was not true of the age of Hergenröther. He went on quietly with his scholarly work, always he presided rather than ruled, he never wielded influence among the Italian cardinals of the Curia. But his importance, behind the scenes, is proved by the anxieties of the workers in the archives lest he die. They knew that the Pope was pressed from other sides, and felt a recurring sense of gratitude to Hergenröther for helping the Pope to set the archives upon a course which they hoped was irreversible. His death made them worry.

A long delay ensued, during which Denifle and Wenzel and Palmieri[24] carried on the now established ways, and protracted discussions took place over the successor. A strong body of local opinion wanted to have an Italian instead of a German. Some wished to be altogether rid of the Austrian Denifle. At last in June 1891 Pope Leo appointed a learned orientalist with small experience of archives, the Augustinian eremite Agostino Ciasca, who was not yet a cardinal. They found Ciasca stricter than Hergenröther in maintaining the formal rules, but had no reason to be dissatisfied. They did not then know that Ciasca went to the cardinals of the Curia and consulted them about the policy of Hergenröther, and received the advice that the policy was wrong and that the archives should not have been opened; and that despite advice of such weight, Pope Leo held on his way.[25] An odd but trivial crisis occurred under the régime of Monsignor Ciasca, when research suggested that the Nonantula *Life* of Pope Hadrian III was worthless, just when the Pope moved to confirm his cult as saint.[26] Ciasca stayed little more than a year and was succeeded by the picturesque Luigi Tripepi (1892–4), not yet a cardinal.

When Tripepi left, Pope Leo once more appointed a cardinal, this time one of his two most famous cardinals. Galimberti's career lay almost wholly in diplomacy. He had a European name for his part in making peace between Bismarck and the Catholic Church. He became prefect of the archives only because he needed an honourable post in Rome. Without experience of libraries, he had no natural inclination to be interested in documents. To recreate a Cardinal-archivist looked like an elevation of the institution. But in real terms it was not. For Galimberti, though a favoured son of the Pope, was deeply distrusted by other Roman cardinals for his radical programme in European politics. The Austrian ambassador said that he was the bête-noir of many of the cardinals. The Hungarian Fraknói fancied that this unusually powerful and energetic man might do them good by his force of mind in the Curia, to achieve what the workers specially wanted, the

opening of the archives in the various separated congregations, not yet part of the Vatican Archives. But Fraknói's hope
was disappointed. Galimberti continued to be used for high
European politics, and sometimes expressed a desire to be
relieved of the post of prefect of the archives, a calling to
which he could give so little time. He died unexpectedly in
1896, after only two years in office.[27]

Though Galimberti was friendly, Fraknói was sorry that
they had not chosen Denifle, and thought that they might.
Perhaps the Pope considered Denifle's pugnacity, or perhaps
his experience of Hergenröther's term of office led him to
think that a German did not easily exert authority among
Italians in the Curia.

To succeed Galimberti in 1896, the Pope appointed another
cardinal, Francesco Segna. Not everyone was pleased at the
choice of another cardinal whose career lay in administration.
But unlike his predecessor, Cardinal Segna had time to take
a lively interest in the archives, and was pleasant and helpful
to the users. They could hardly bless him enough for one
innovation. The winter of 1900 was so cold that students at the
archives could not write. Wenzel applied to Cardinal Segna,
who told the Pope; and at last the old doctrine that risk of fire
must ban heat was overcome, the boiler was sited a long way
away, and hot water radiators appeared in the students' room
at the archives.[28] At last men could work during winter without
freezing.

Through these too frequent changes Denifle and Wenzel
were allowed to continue the general policy framed by
Hergenröther.

For the first time they began to be mightily helped by an
officer of the library next door. Not until 1895 did the German
Jesuit Franz Ehrle become prefect of the Vatican Library. But
for a decade before that time he helped the archives, knowing
that the borderland between archives and library was more
blurred than men in the separate institutions supposed. This
librarian was a rare archivist and palaeographer. Under his
stimulus Pope Leo created (1892) the reference library often

called the Leonine Library, available for workers in both library and archives. This new library was stocked with gifts from the countries which sent workers to library or archives. Its opening was Ehrle's first big achievement. It eased the tasks of students working with Denifle or Wenzel. Students of today can hardly imagine how without it they could do such work.

Denifle was baptized Joseph but took the names Henry Suso when he joined the Dominicans because he was already engaged in the study of the mystics of medieval Germany. He was the son of a village organist and schoolmaster in the Upper Tyrol. He became professor in the Dominican college of Graz (1870–80) until his order sent him to Rome to help the new edition of St Thomas Aquinas, planned in consequence of the impetus given to Thomist studies by Pope Leo XIII. Hence he was known in Rome when Balan fell from grace, and became sub-archivist from 1883 until his death in 1905 while he travelled northward to receive an honorary degree from the University of Cambridge. Unlike Wenzel, who had no desire to be a historian, Denifle seized with passion the chance of historical work given to him by his place in the archives. Turning from mysticism he dedicated himself to a fundamental work on the origins of the medieval universities, and then the Chartulary of the University of Paris. In an important sense he was less practical use to the workers than Wenzel, for he had not much time to continue the very necessary ordering of the archives. But being more learned, and dedicated to scholarship, and the stronger personality, he helped enquirers with rare information and was seen by them as leader of the staff. He was pugnacious by nature, friends called him *volcanic*, a *Titan*. They said that they were never allowed to forget that he was born a Tyrolean peasant. On an occasion when one of Sickel's assistants committed a peccadillo, Sickel was glad that a long table divided him (Sickel) from a purple-faced Denifle while reproaches were heaped upon his head. Denifle always felt, and behaved as though he felt, like a sentry at his post; valiant for truth, a watchdog for the interests of the

Catholic Church. His panegyrist said of him after his death, 'He was the leader of a fight, like Judas Maccabaeus'. But the full range of his pugnacity was known only to a few of the workers in the archives and a few authors whose books he so reviewed as to annihilate. When he published the first volume of his onslaught on Luther in 1904, and set ablaze the academic community, he surprised the general public. Some fancied that he was violent against Luther because he resembled Luther in character. Not one of his chief works was complete when he died. But meanwhile he gave new impetus to the history of medieval universities, of mysticism and the study of Luther. Off duty, he uttered sharp witticisms in a south German dialect. Despite a gaunt and bony face with heavy spectacles, and an appearance which resembled the Inquisitor of legend, he enjoyed a pot of beer and a touch of bawdy. His room was littered with a chaos of books and papers. There he could fascinate the serious enquirer with his information. Haller looked back upon his interviews with Denifle, in that untidiest of studies, as some of the best moments of his time in Rome. After the reign of Balan, Fraknói once called the reign of Denifle the golden age of the archives.[29]

Denifle was not a man who thought everything in the archives suitable to publish. He found a letter from Pope Gregory XIII's cardinal to the nuncio in Spain concerning Queen Elizabeth of England. He saw it as a singularly unfortunate letter, since it contains a blessing on tyrannicide. It was supposed that the idea passed over his mind that things would be better for the Church if it were destroyed. But he was said to have said, with resignation, that as God willed the document to survive until now, destruction would not be appropriate. Before many years passed, the letter was published.[30]

The militant Tyrolese was not comfortable with Sickel, himself easy to rouse. Though Sickel admired what Denifle did and was, he preferred to avoid meetings over business, knowing that between them sparks were quick to fly. In the eighteen-nineties they had a tremendous battle, when Cardinal Galimberti gave Sickel a privilege which Denifle thought unwarranted. But towards the end of their lives Sickel happened to meet Denifle in Salzburg just after Denifle published his battery against Luther. Feeling was running so high that Sickel's host asked him whether he would prefer to avoid the encounter. Sickel went straight to Denifle and shook his hand, and the pair of old warriors fell to reminiscence of days in Rome.[31] It was characteristic of their personal difficulty that before they began to reminisce, Sickel insisted on making clear what he thought about Luther.

Pietro Wenzel looked nothing like an Inquisitor. He had a rubicund fat face, and an open friendly manner. Occasionally the workers fancied a touch of the pedant in him, and when they argued about candidates who might succeed to the headship of the archives, they were inclined to rule him out as not quite possessing the stature. But because he had no pretensions to scholarship, he worked steadily away at the indexes, trying all the time to make documents easier to find, and the archives less like a heap into which men dipped fingers hopefully. Being an Italian, and possessing Italian charm, he was at home with the members of the Curia, and among the archivists came closest to Pope Leo XIII.

The Benedictine, Gregorio Palmieri, though he remained at the archives till he resigned in 1895, and wrote a Latin guide to their use, was never so important or helpful as Denifle and Wenzel. He was an Italian who disapproved the Austrian invasion of the archives, had a touch of the morose in his manner, and was regarded by Sickel as an antagonist. His influence was weakened because during 1887 he was detected after releasing a document which, though long before the date of 1815 when the archives were still closed, was regarded as contrary to religious interests. In an uncatalogued volume he found a writing accusing Giordano Bruno of error in Catholic faith. Not only was Giordano Bruno burnt as a heretic in 1600, but the antipapal forces of the eighteen-eighties used his death as a stick with which to beat the Papacy and to show how, as in the trial of Galileo, priests stopped scientists by force. Pope Leo felt sensitive, and wished nothing published. When

Gregorio Palmieri found this unknown document, he was excited. Though he had not known enough about early medieval manuscripts to recognize the *Liber Diurnus* when Sickel asked for copies of early scripts, he knew enough to know that he had an important paper. He gave a copy to a Benedictine colleague at St Paul's outside the walls, and talked of it to an Italian professor. This knowledge came back to the archives, and behind the scenes caused turmoil. Pietro Wenzel told Pope Leo XIII who gave summary orders. Palmieri received a severe rebuke and Cardinal Hergenröther got back the illicit copy. An Italian who three years later applied to see the document was refused.[32]

The historian must continually remind himself that such exceptions were not confined to the Vatican Archives. Even in 1916 the German Foreign Office ruled that to publish the political testament of King Frederick the Great of Prussia was inopportune. The Italian government long refused access to its state archives, and its agents tried to prevent historians getting too near the papers of Cavour, or of the royal house. 'It would not be right,' said an Italian prime minister in 1912, 'to have beautiful legends discredited by historical criticism.'[33]

Piece by piece, the exceptions at the Vatican grew rarer. An important sign of Pope Leo's stability was the brief commending the first volume of the publication by the Görres Society of the minutes of the Council of Trent. The atmosphere had changed from the time when a commission stopped Augustin Theiner from publishing precisely these documents. In this brief Pope Leo referred back to that attitude towards history which seventeen years before he showed in his Letter to the Three Cardinals.[34]

On 5 May 1902, Fraknói arranged that the Pope should receive the heads of the national research institutes and their colleagues or assistants. On a Sunday at 11 a.m. Fraknói led twenty-one students to a hall, and then the Pope's little white-robed figure came in and despite his ninety-two years climbed a low throne. Fraknói read a solemn speech in Latin thanking the Pope for the magnanimous opening of the archives. In his deep bass voice, Pope Leo replied with equal formality in Latin, reading from a paper which he was handed. Haller remembered nothing but vague generalities without content, Pastor heard him say *splendore veritatis gaudet ecclesia*, the Church takes pleasure in the light of truth. Then Fraknói presented them one by one, in alphabetical order of countries. Pastor, as Austria was first, received from the Pope a warm gesture and greeting. Then the head of the Prussian (Borussian) institute, Schulte, came forward and was received in cold silence. Now came to kneel the head of the Ecole française, Louis Duchesne, ablest historian then working in Rome and disliked or feared by members of the Curia, partly for sardonic wit and partly for his attitude to French politics. The Pope's manner showed displeasure. Still kneeling, arms crossed on his breast, Duchesne began in a dull voice, 'Holy Father. By now we have published eighty thousand documents from the Vatican Archives and' – he paused, and made a despairing gesture, and then changed to a mournful voice – 'up to now not a single document that could hurt the Holy See!' For a moment Pope Leo was taken aback. Then his face cleared and he began to laugh. The laughter was infectious, everyone started to laugh, even the officers joined, and Haller remembered such a reverberation of laughter as that hall of solemnities could hardly ever have heard.

Fraknói made most of the other presentations in an embarrassing silence.[35]

But the Pope was old, and died next year, and the historians again were anxious. Even before he died they were disturbed at what might follow. Pastor delayed writing his next volume, for which the materials were ready, so that he could spend the time collecting materials for later volumes – in fear that those materials might no longer be accessible.[36] Leo's successor Pius X was a good and pious man but no intellectual. Six weeks after the election Cardinal Segna the Cardinal-archivist was assured by the new Pope that he should continue in the old ways. On 17 October 1903 Pastor was received by Pius X and offered him the fourth edition of his first volume. By previous agreement

with his friend Paul Kehr, he asked Pius X to continue the
freedom which Leo XIII introduced to the archives. Pius X
said 'It was a great act of the dead Pope to open the archives
to all scholars. If we keep it like that the Church can only
benefit. We are not to be afraid of truth. In your book you
showed the human infirmities of Popes and you were right. That
cannot do harm. These infirmities are like passing clouds, after
which the sun shines more brightly.'[37] Historians were
nevertheless surprised and pleased. Fraknói came from Hungary to Rome not long after Pius X was elected, and could
not help a cry of *praise be* when he found that everything in
the archives went on 'in the old ways'.[38] Even eleven years
later, in 1914, Pastor again took the trouble to ask for the same
assurance from the next Pope, Benedict XV. The first Pope
whom Pastor felt no need to encourage was Pius XI at his
accession in 1922; for Pius XI was once librarian of the Ambrosian Library in Milan and later prefect of the Vatican Library.
But even before the appearance of a scholar-Pope, change
was rapid. On 16 April 1920 Pastor recorded that the placard
of excommunication against persons entering the archives
disappeared. Cardinal Gasquet, who became Cardinal-
archivist in 1917 and in addition Cardinal-librarian two years
later,[39] achieved this ritual relaxation. Gasquet achieved something more. When Pastor finally got freedom to work through
all the catalogues of the archives, he followed a trail about Pope
Alexander VI Borgia which he hardly expected. He had
received permission to work at the registers of that Pope, and
wrote his famous volume on the acts which he found. But as
he worked through the catalogues, he found the existence of
a group of documents called 'reserved acts of Alexander VI',
which were preserved separately in the 'Archivio di Castello',
that is, documents which before the French Revolution were
kept for close security in the Castel Sant' Angelo. These were
the remains of the Pope's private correspondence during the
years 1493–4; a little later Pastor found that these reserved acts
contained letters from Lucrezia Borgia to the Pope, letters of
Vanozza Catanei, and even letters from and to Julia Farnese.

In May 1921 Pastor, now ambassador at the Vatican for the new and minuscule Austria, won the two final steps in this history.

On 14 May 1921 Angelo Mercati was copying down for Pastor the letters of Lucrezia Borgia.

Two days later, 16 May, Pastor became the first person not an archivist, and not the roaming Englishman Joseph Stevenson, to visit all the rooms of the Vatican Secret Archives, and to see with surprise the beauty of the frescoes, dating from early in the seventeenth century, which so few eyes had been permitted to see.[40] He worked at the history of the popes for forty-two years before he could visit all the rooms where his principal documents were stored, before he saw what Joseph Stevenson freely saw while the archives were shut closer than at any other time in their history.

One week later, 23 May 1921, Cardinal Gasquet agreed that all the letters to and from Pope Alexander VI, even the letters with Julia Farnese, could be published. Pastor had not felt certain about Gasquet's attitude. He wrote in his diary for that day, '*All the truth is now his watchword too.*'[41]

7

Epilogue

The archives were open because European public opinion
made it impossible to keep them shut. But the popes had not
the habit of paying excessive attention to European public
opinion, and Leo XIII's act of faith was one of the most
liberal acts in an illiberal century, and was sustained under
pressure and counter-advice. The policy was proved correct
by its results; from the mass of impartial enquiry which access
permitted to scholars, non-Catholic or Catholic; from the
steady desire of the archivists themselves, and the scholarly
work which they promoted – Denifle, Wenzel, Ehrle, Mercati
to name only the chief; and from the general consequences
of new attitudes in Catholic historical scholarship.

The opening of the archives brought general understanding, and new confidence among instructed non-Catholics that
the Catholic Church cared about truth. It also enabled many
important advances in history. But it did not achieve what the
Three Cardinals, in first flush of enthusiasm after 1883,
predicted or hoped. In the days when the Vatican Secret
Archives were secret, and when Marini or Theiner mysteri-
ously conjured unknown documents from behind a door over
which ran the menace of excommunication, legend or hope
magnified the treasure. When the mystery was dispelled, men
found that few documents existed from the time before 1198
when Pope Innocent III began to establish order, and that
even in the later Middle Ages or Counter-Reformation more
rewarding documents might lie elsewhere. Those who made
the best use of the opened Vatican Archives, like Ludwig von
Pastor or Paul Kehr, found that they spent as much or more

effort in Italian or German or Spanish archives. A time came when some students of medieval Europe aspersed the Vatican Archives and said that they disappointed; that they were no use till Innocent III, that much was missing in the later Middle Ages, that Rome ceased to be of importance in European politics after the Thirty Years War; that even in the age of Reformation and Counter-Reformation, they only confirmed what was known. All this was an exaggerated swing of the pendulum. The archive contained treasure which will not be exhausted yet for many decades. Legend, and lock and key, and Theiner's methods, created a fantasy.

This inflation made the task of the national historical institutes more difficult. The Ecole française sent Elie Berger to do the first work in a mighty series of registers. The Austrians and Prussians founded their institutes with the special object of exploiting the riches of the Vatican Archives. Many decades later the goals at which the institutes aimed have not been reached. This was partly because they met the difficulty from which the commission of Three Cardinals suffered. They needed students to study documents, the students must be good; if they were good, they were soon called away to be archivists or librarians or professors in their own lands; new and inexperienced students must be trained. But aside from this practical difficulty, the expectations of the eighteen-eighties were pitched too high. Like the officers of the Public Record Office when they ordered Joseph Stevenson to copy the documents of several centuries, they planned before they knew what there was to plan.

Still, an enthusiasm which brought to publication such a series as the reports of the nuncios from all over Europe, to mention but one among the endeavours, will rouse gratitude for the faith in which it was undertaken.

A common enquiry into history transcended religious disagreement. The nineteenth century, realistic about men, did not believe that a historian could lack bias. Even Pope Leo XIII seemed to suspect Sickel of losing his Protestant faith because in history he proved something to the advantage of the popes.

Whether or not a historian can lack bias, that attitude at least became an anachronism. Cardinal Franz Ehrle said to the Protestant historian Lietzmann when he was working at Roman archives, 'We are all servants of a single truth.'[1]

Not all was done that everyone wanted. The archives remained not only a treasure-house of history, but the working papers of a government. Governments keep their papers hidden for a time. This time diminished, with many governments, during the middle twentieth century. But with certain exceptions permitted for special reasons, the Vatican Archives remained closed for longer – Gasquet thought that he achieved a victory when (1920–1) he persuaded the authorities that the period of open access be extended from 1815 to 1830. Later they came to 1846, then to 1878 – but the period of closure was long because the memory of a Church is longer than the memory of a State. This situation has not pleased all modern historians, and we must hope that soon provision will be made for opening to 1903 if not to 1914 or 1922. The old subjection of the archives to the office of Secretary of State has demerits in the modern world; for Secretaries of State usually mind less about history than those in charge of archives.

Pastor concerned himself over the archives of the Inquisition. In Paris after the Battle of Waterloo Monsignor Marino Marini destroyed a number of volumes of papers from the Inquisition. But many volumes of trials remained. By the end of the nineteenth century the prohibited access to them became as interesting as the once prohibited access to the trial of Galileo.

Early in 1902 Pastor tried to get leave to see the papers. He was very strong in the Vatican, receiving a new brief from Pope Leo XIII that spring. In March that year he heard a story from one of his reliable acquaintances that the Dominicans were against Pastor because they disliked his treatment of the friar Savonarola in the volume on Pope Alexander VI.[2] All through the year 1902 dragged the negotiations about getting inside the archive of the Holy Office. After fourteen months Pastor was weary and hopeless. On 20 January 1903 he recorded in his diary:

Van Rossum, Redemptorist, archivist of the Holy Office, said to me today that all my efforts would be in vain; the cardinals would let me see a single document if I asked for it, but not a volume of decrees. How can I use the documents when I do not know what is there? I see it is all useless. I will say nothing harsh or dishonouring about the Inquisition in my *History of the Popes*; but they cannot defend themselves, for I have not the documents to make a judgment. May the enemies of the Church never seize the archives of the Inquisition! If they do, the documents will be used to discredit the Church, whereas they ought to be put in true light by a Catholic.

It later turned out that Gasquet achieved something with archives of the Inquisition. In 1896 Gasquet was researching on materials concerning the validity of Anglican orders. He asked the Pope for authority to see the papers of the Inquisition. Pope Leo consented. The archivist at the Inquisition took no notice. For two months, though armed with the Pope's permission, Gasquet could not get in. So he wrote to the Pope and said that he could not do his work and would go away. At once the Pope summoned him. 'Why do you write to me like that?' 'I had to,' said Gasquet. 'I thought your Holiness was master of the archive of the Inquisition. I was wrong.' The Pope then caused the acts, which Gasquet needed, to be brought out for his use.

In the age of Theiner, Lord Acton believed that archives were the key to authentic history. Write the history from original documents, not from the printed sources, then we shall get to things as they really happened. The doctrine had a truth with which no serious modern historian could dispense. But it was less all-embracing as truth than appeared to the enthusiasts of that age when the archives of Europe were first made easy of access. In the notes of Acton's old age, we find doubt creeping in.

Archives are bulky, history is selective. Early in his career Pastor realized that what he tried to do was impossible if it meant using all the archives; for the archives were 'an ocean' in which men lost their way, and he felt like a man trying to scoop out the sea with a shell. *What's the use of a pen here? You need a thousand pens.* Late in Pastor's life a hostile critic accused him of failing to 'exhaust' the Vatican Secret Archives. He smiled at the charge. 'Right enough. Ten men could not exhaust them. They will not be exhausted for a century. You can only select what is important.'[3]

Acton saw, much earlier, that the weight of paper could mislead. Printed books may be selective. But documents preserved in an archive are also selected in their origin. They are themselves to be distrusted, because of their nature and the gaps. The weight of paper makes the selection at once more necessary and more difficult. Those who collect paper often need to keep it because of a quarrel, a controversy, a discreditable incident where the letters exchanged must be preserved as protection or guide in future trouble. Therefore to publish archives is sometimes like publishing the seamy side, even like selecting the seamy side, and so unbalancing the impartial scales of history. 'What people conceal is not their best deeds and motives but their worst. What archives reveal is the wickedness of man. It [*sic*] destroys idols and scatters theories.'[4]

I am the fortunate possessor of that copy of the *Life of Cardinal Manning* by Edmund Sheridan Purcell, which formerly belonged to the founder of this lectureship, Herbert Hensley Henson. I am able therefore to follow the underlinings, blue-pencillings, symbols, interjections which marked Henson's excited interest and at times enjoyment of scandal as he read the book. Part of the notoriety of that book consisted in the way its author mishandled his sources as well as his theme. But a still larger part of the notoriety came because the author published confidential letters only thirty years after they were written; and they happened to be letters of such a nature (being mainly written by a complex character, George Talbot) that the impact of their publication did as much to hurt history as to help. On the face of it, anything new printed helps the historian. But if one group of letters alone is printed, and these written from a partisan or eccentric point of view, while all other relevant documents are kept under lock and key, the progress of history is hindered for a time, since the historian is blinded by the sources which he possesses and has no means of correcting his blindness. This is an argument for publishing more archives, not less. But the custody of the Manning papers by Manning's heirs at Bayswater has been so odd that more than eighty years later it is still impossible to get the letters, printed by Purcell, into proper context and focus. Henson's marginalia on the book show that he was hardly aware of the need for future corrective. The comments about Purcell's *Life* in Henson's private journal (4 November 1941) show him at first without suspicion that the narrative might one day need reconsidering; until four days later, after reading ('squandering hours') on four other narrative sources about the same theme, two of them Catholic and two anti-Catholic, he reached the verdict that the story was not only squalid but *muddled*; and the word *muddled* is the confession of the historical mind that all is not yet well with the evidence which he finds.

Henson was familiar with the workings of the world. He knew that in a college the bursar's safe keeps the records of quarrels in the society; and therefore the danger always exists that some superficial historian of the next century will write a history of the college solely out of the archives in the bursar's safe, and infer that the history of the college is nothing but the crimes and follies of the Fellows. If that were what were meant by history then it could not do what Henson in his old age hoped that it might do. It would lie only on the hard surface of mankind.

This was the truth which lay under Acton's perception, late in his life, that what archives reveal is the wickedness of man.

And then, Acton reflected as he prepared for Oxford University the Romanes Lecture which he was never able to deliver, *The dust of archives blots out ideas*. The pile of paper could hamper the reflection of the historian if he allowed himself to sink within its comfortable but sometimes trivial certainties. Pope Pius XI, who was an Alpinist as well as a scholar, once said to Pastor, 'You were never a climber, because you spent all your time sitting in archives.'[5] The Pope perhaps intended to apply a shrewd and smiling comment not only to Pastor's body. The *History of the Popes* has a mass of valuable information which the author was able to arrange and narrate while sustaining the interest of the reader. But it suffers because he never took time to stand back and consider.

Still, whether or not we consider, we cannot do without the archives if we want truth. The risk that Acton saw has to be run.

In his *Italienische Reise* of 1823–5 the Protestant Pertz wrote that the disclosure of the documents would help the popes because it would show the European or world-stature of the office. 'The best defence of the Papacy is to show how it works. If weaknesses appear, you get a better judgment out of history if the facts are known than if they are so concealed that all facts are suspect.' A quarter of a century later the Protestant Böhmer longed for a new Pope who would think of history as 'a light from heaven for dark places'. Though Leo XIII was no historian, that was how he came to think about history because all about him he saw propaganda claiming to derive from history, and had faith that true history must drive out false. The cardinal of the twentieth century who did not like men to write frankly about bad popes, and who said *first charity then truth, even in history*, had an ecclesiastical idea of the meaning of the word *charity*.

The diploma which Leo XIII awarded to the graduates of the school for palaeography which he founded in connection with the archives, was given a motto, which fitly closes this study: *nihil est quod ecclesiae ab inquisitione veri metuatur* – the Church has nothing to fear from the quest for truth.

Notes

CHAPTER 1

1 D. McElrath (ed.), *Lord Acton: the Decisive Decade, 1864–74* (Louvain 1970), 131.

2 L. E. Boyle, *A Survey of the Vatican Archives and of its Medieval Holdings* (Pontifical Institute of Medieval Studies, Toronto 1972), 37. This is the best of modern guides. It has not wholly displaced the classic K. A. Fink and the excellent articles by Leslie Macfarlane – designed for students of British history but also of general help – see the Select Bibliography.

3 Ludwig von Pastor, *The History of the Popes from the Close of the Middle Ages*, Eng. trans., IX (London 1938–53), 414.

4 Aubrey Diller, 'A Greek manuscript strayed from the Vatican Library', *Bodleian Library Record*, VII (1962–7), 39–42. It is Ms. Barocci, 142. The manuscript was in the Vatican Library in 1524 and next appeared when the Barocci manuscripts were acquired by an English bookseller 1628–9 and bought by the Chancellor of Oxford University to present to the library. Though the manuscript did not certainly vanish at the sack of Rome, that was the easiest time for loot. Cf. also J. Bignami Odier, *La Bibliothèque Vaticane de Sixte IV à Pie IX* (Vatican City 1973), 42; Pastor, *History of the Popes*, IX, 415 n. 1; *Summary Catalogue of Western Manuscripts in the Bodleian Library*, II, 3ff.

5 Pastor, *History of the Popes*. XVI, 409.

6 Pastor, *History of the Popes*, XII, 546–7; XVII, 132–3; Julius III to Marcello Cervini, 24 February 1550, in Pastor, XIII, 433, Appendix 5.

7 Pastor, *History of the Popes*, XIX, 275; XXII, 407; E. Müntz, *La Bibliothèque du Vatican au XVIe Siècle* (Paris 1886), 131ff.

8 Franciscus Schottus, *Itinerari italiae rerumque romanarum libri tres*, 4th edn (Antwerp 1625), 277.

9 Pastor, *History of the Popes*, XXII, 407; XXIV, 447.

10 Heinsius to Queen Christina, Venice, 10 June 1652; cf. 9 February 1652–3; in P. Burman, *Sylloges epistolarum*, IV (5 vols., Leyden 1727), 743–4.

11ʹ Pastor, *History of the Popes*, XXIV, 447.

12 Boyle, *Survey of the Vatican Archives*, 10.

13 Pastor, *History of the Popes*, XXV, 101–2.

14 Pastor, *History of the Popes*, XXX, 119–20.

15 Leopold von Ranke, *History of the Popes*, Eng. trans. (London 1913), II, 348; III, 290; Pastor, *History of the Popes*, XXIX, 183; XXX, 351–2.

16 L. P. Gachard, *Les Archives du Vatican* (Brussels 1874), 41.

17 *Lexikon für Theologie und Kirche*, 3rd edn (Freiburg-im-Breisgau 1957–68), *s.v.* Cervini; *Conc. Trident.* (Görres Soc.) X, xv–xxix; H. Jedin, *History of the Council of Trent*, Eng. trans., II (1961), 515–16.

18 Boyle, *Survey of the Vatican Archives*, 10–11.

19 Pastor, *History of the Popes*, XXXIV, 390.

20 *Diarium* in I. P. Dengel, *Die politische und kirchliche Tätigkeit des Mgr Josef Garampi in Deutschland 1761–1763* (Rome 1905), 3; and for Garampi's lists see *Studi e testi* XLV (1926); L. Pásztor, 'Per la storia dell'Archivio Segreto Vaticano nei Secoli XVII–XVIII', *Archivio della società Romana di storia patria*, XCI (1968), 237ff.; and Irmtraut Lindeck-Pozza, 'Der Präfekt des Vatikanischen Archivs, Conte Giuseppe Garampi, in Wien 1772', *Römische Historische Mitteilungen*, XVII (1975), 77–102.

21 Pastor, *History of the Popes*, XXXVIII, 177, 365. Benedict XIV created a Saxon vicar-apostolic in 1743, *Lexikon für Theologie und Kirche*, IX, 201.

CHAPTER 2

1 M. Marini, 'Memorie storiche dell'occupazione e restituzione degli Archivii della S. Sede', in *Regestum Clementis V*, I (Rome 1885), prolegomena; L. de Lisle, *Journal des Savants*, 1892, 438ff.; H. Leclercq, in *Dictionnaire d'archéologie chrétienne et de liturgie*, *s.v.* Gaetano Marini.

2 The golden bulls are studied and illustrated by P. Sella, *Inventari dell'Archivio Segreto Vaticano: le Bolle d'Oro dell'Archivio* (Vatican City 1934).

3 J. Schmidlin, *Papstgeschichte der neuesten Zeit*, I (Munich 1933), xi.

4 Marini, 'Memorie', cclxviiiff.; R. Ritzler, 'Der Verschleppung der päpstlichen Archiv unter Napoleon I', *Römische Historische Mitteilungen*, VI–VII (1962–4), 149ff.

5 Promemoria, Archivio degli Affari Ecclesiastici, 11 July 1816; printed Ritzler, 180–1.

6 Report of Antonio Benvenuti at Civita Vecchia, 4 October 1817, to Cardinal Consalvi; printed Ritzler, 184–5, no. 45.

7 Marini to Cardinal Consalvi, 7 March 1816; printed Ritzler, 163. He was not the only person so engaged during those years. In 1809 Llorente, who was an ex-officer of the Spanish Inquisition, destroyed documents of the Inquisition, preserving those which he thought to be historically important. See his *Histoire critique de l'Inquisition d'Espagne*, 2nd ed., IV (Paris 1818), 145.

8 Marini to the Duc de Richelieu, Secretary of State, 23 July 1817; printed Ritzler, 186–7, no. 50.

9 Laborde, cited Acton, Inaugural, 107; Daunou's instructions of 1 October 1810 ('Direct your attention to what could serve to uncover the ambitious policy of the Curia') and of 3 January 1811, in *Archivalische Zeitschrift*, V (1880), 82.

10 Carl von Gebler, *Galileo Galilei and the Roman Curia*, Eng. trans. (London 1879), Appendix, 320–2.

11 By Angelo Mercati, *Atti della Pontificia Accademia delle Scienze Nuove Lincei*, A. LXXX, Session I, 19 December 1926; letters from the nuncio in Vienna enclosing the papers by courier, 6 October 1843.

12 To Biot, cf. R. R. Madden, *Galileo and the Inquisition* (London, Dublin 1863), 54–5.

13 G. H. Pertz, *Autobiography and Letters*, ed. Leonora Pertz, Eng. trans. (London 1894), 37.

14 Original in G. H. Pertz, *Italienische Reise* (Hanover 1824), 29. Pertz's copies were edited at last by C. Rodenberg, in *Monumenta Germaniae Historica* (1883ff.). Cf. the use of this text by J. F. Böhmer in a letter of 10 November 1855 to Beda Dudík, printed in Johannes Janssen, *J. F. Böhmers Leben, Briefe und kleinere Schriften*, III (Freiburg-im-Breisgau 1868), 159, no. 387.

15 Pertz, *Autobiography*, Eng. trans., 46.

16 The British agent in Rome was William Hamilton, welcome to the Curia because he helped with the recovery of works of art from France. The papers were transferred to the British Museum by order of Sir James Graham. Part of them arrived there on 1 May 1843, the remainder on 4 July 1845. Copy of W. R. Hamilton's explanatory letter of 19 November 1842 in Acton MSS., General Correspondence *s.v.* Romilly, Cambridge University Library.

17 Pertz, *Italienische Reise*, 25; for other criticism see (e.g.) Franz Palacký, *Literarische Reise nach Italien im Jahre 1837* (Prague 1838), 3–7, 53–4.

18 Janssen, *Böhmers Leben*, I, 219–20, 326ff., 335; III, 159; and cf. I. P. Dengel, *Mittheilungen des Instituts für Österreichische Geschichtsforschung*, XXV (Innsbruck 1904), 311–12, especially 312 n. 2.

19 Gebler, *Galileo*, Eng. trans., 341–2.

20 G. M. Trevelyan, *Garibaldi's Defence of the Roman Republic*, I (London 1907), 102.

21 Published as 'Il processo Galileo', *Rivista Europea*, III (1870); see his preface for his experiences; and Gebler, *Galileo*, Eng. trans., 339ff. French troops again occupied the buildings of the Holy Office early in August 1851 and the archives must again be moved temporarily, this time into the Vatican. For the letters of Marino Marini to Cardinal Antonelli showing his surprise, when restored to the control of the archives after the revolution, that they had suffered no loss, see the documents cited by Angelo Mercati, *Studi e testi*, CI (1942), 15–16.

22 M. Marini, 'Storia dell'autografo manuscritto del processo di Galileo', in *Galileo e l'Inquisizione* (Rome 1850), 143ff.

23 Madden, *Galileo and the Inquisition*, 58.

24 Marini, *Galileo*, 42, 98–100; and cf. the animadversions of Gebler, *Galileo*, Eng. trans., 221; Gherardi, *Rivista Europea*, III (1870), 9; *Civiltà Cattolica*, November 1850, 166ff.

25 Gachard, *Les Archives du Vatican*, 1–2. This did not mean that volumes might not be fetched out for approved readers. In the same year that Gachard felt frustrated, Marini allowed Beda Dudík, sent by the government of Moravia, to see fifty-nine volumes of papal registers – the largest number hitherto released. On this evidence Dudík wrote the first study of the papal registers. We have a letter from Marino Marini to Theiner (13 May 1853, *Carte Theiner*, 3) saying that he has worked for Dudík but thinks him not at all satisfied. Dudík on his side published fulsome gratitude to Marino Marini, cf. Dudík, *Iter romanum*, II (Vienna 1855), 50; in the Vatican Archive is an effusive letter of thanks from Dudík to Marino Marini, 16 October 1853, Vienna (*Carte Theiner* 1/929). Gachard later paid a fruitful visit to the Vatican (1867–8).

CHAPTER 3

1 Cf. Viennot to Acton, Paris, 17 July 1869, Acton Papers, Box 10, Cambridge University Library.

2 Theiner to Acton, 13 December 1865, Acton Papers, Box 10.

3 *Die Einführung der erzwungenen Ehelosigkeit bei den christlichen Geistlichen und ihre Folgen* (Altenberg 1828).

4 K. Hoffmann, *Lexikon für Theologie und Kirche*, s.v. Theiner, Johann Anton; Achille Mauri, in *Archivio storico italiano*, XXI (1875), 351.

5 *Commentatio de Romanorum Pontificum epistolarum decretalium antiquis collectionibus et de Gregorii IX Pontificis Maximi decretalium codice.*

6 By a French title. The original was the preface to his *Geschichte der geistlichen Bildungsanstalten* (Mainz 1835), preface dated 13 November 1833. Interesting testimony to the influence of this preface in a letter from Martino Mielli of the Oratory to Theiner from Venice, 13 September 1841, *Carte Theiner*, 3/318; cf. also letters from Dr Russell of Maynooth, *Carte Theiner*, 3/1013 and ff. As early as 1834 the Jesuits at St Ignazio and at the Gesù read Theiner's preface in the refectory and were reported as much pleased, cf. Sophia Hohenlohe to Theiner, 27 September 1834, *Carte Theiner*, 2/438. For the relationship to Johann Adam Möhler at Tübingen during these years, see S. Lösch, *Prof. Dr Adam Gengler* (Würzburg 1963), 197ff.

7 Newman's *Letters and Diaries*, ed. C. S. Dessain, XII (London 1962), 62.

8 Marini to Theiner, 2 November 1836, *Carte Theiner*, 3/165; Theiner being at Propaganda.

9 e.g. Marini to Theiner, 26 April 1846, *Carte Theiner*, 3/175, on formulas for anathemas, e.g. Urban VI's bulls against Clement VII.

10 Marini to Theiner, 20 June 1846, *Carte Theiner*, 3/177.

11 Hermann Gisiger, *P. Theiner und die Jesuiten* (Mannheim 1875), 27.

12 *Carte Theiner*, 3/208; letter of appointment 29 November 1855, in VSA, Secretary of State, 1855/67; Pope's request (28 November 1855), in H. Jedin, 'Gustav Hohenlohe an Augustin Theiner 1850–70', *Römische Quartalschrift*, LXVI (1971), 176.

13 *Archivio Particolare di Pio Nono*, no, 1380.

14 Gisiger, *Theiner*, 18.

15 Gisiger, *Theiner*, 47–8. He discussed Ranke with the King of Bavaria. Theiner said that Ranke had done less than justice to Pope Gregory XIII, Acton, *Historical Essays and Studies*, ed. J. N. Figgis & R. V. Laurence (London 1907), 358.

16 Alois Flir, *Briefe aus Rom*, 2nd edn, ed. L. Rapp (Innsbruck 1864), 131; a letter of 2 July 1858.

17 *The Ring and the Book*, I.

18 So Tosti in Theodor von Sickel, *Römische Erinnerungen*, ed. L. Santifaller (Vienna 1947), 185.

19 For Munch, cf. U. Berlière, 'Aux Archives Vaticanes', *Revue Bénédictine*, XX (1903), 132–4; Sickel, *Römische Erinnerungen*, 213; Friedensburg. The Munch case was made remarkable by a peculiar condition in Munch's instructions. At Rome in 1860 he made a memorandum about the Vatican Archives and sent it to the Academy of Sciences in Christiania. When he returned to Norway he deposited it in the Norwegian State Archives with the instruction that it be not published during Theiner's life-time. This instruction became known when Gustav Storm

published the memorandum (Christiania, 1876) and S. Löwenfeld gave it a German translation in *Archivalische Zeitschrift*, IV (1879), 66, 149. Because the instruction was odd, and because it appeared in the years after Theiner's death when rumours of his misconduct were widespread, it gave rise to the guess that Theiner broke the rules of the Vatican Archive in Munch's favour. Internal evidence of the memorandum shows only that Theiner was generous in allowing Munch access to numbers of documents, not at all that he misbehaved in his duty as prefect of the archives.

20 Cf. Jedin, *Historisches Jahrbuch*, LXVI (1971), 175.

21 For the quotation, see the texts printed by (e.g.) Carl von Gebler, *Die Acten des Galilei'schen Processes* (Stuttgart 1877), 112, 114.

22 Theiner to Antonelli, 22 October 1857; 30 June 1858; VSA, Secretary of State 1858/67/31–5. For the Austrian side of the experience with Kopp, see Walter Goldinger, 'Österreich und die Eröffnung des Vatikanischen Archivs', *Archivalische Zeitschrift*, XLVII (1951), 24.

23 *Carte Theiner*, 2/776.

24 *Carte Theiner*, 2/780.

25 Cf. Secretary of State, Rubricella 1870, no. 58164.

26 Amusingly described by Gebler, *Galileo*, Eng. trans., 326ff. Pastor, *History of the Popes*, XXIX, 58, believed that Galileo knew how persons over the age of seventy were no longer subjected to torture and so he was immune from this penalty.

CHAPTER 4

1 So in the argument *De auxiliis*; cf. H. Jedin, *Das Konzil von Trient: ein Überblick über die Erforschung seiner Geschichte* (*Storia e letteratura* XIX, Rome 1948), 18–19.

2 Jedin, *Erforschung*, 138–9.

3 Hutchison of London Oratory to Theiner, 16 August 1852, *Carte Theiner*, 2/470.

4 Acton's 1857 journal; printed by H. Butterfield, *Cambridge Historical Journal*, VIII (1944–6), 190.

5 VSA, Secretary of State, 1858/67, Theiner to Antonelli from Florence.

6 A. Sala, *Documenti circa la vita e le gesta di S. Carlo Borromeo*, III (Milan 1861), 14 n. 2.

7 Cardinal Antonelli to the Bishop of Trent, 22 June 1857: Secretary of State, 1858/67/13.

8 Ignaz von Döllinger, *Ungedruckte Berichte und Tagebücher zur Geschichte des Concils von Trient*, I (Nördlingen 1876), xii–xiii; Jedin, *Erforschung*, 181–2.

9 Theiner's receipt to Hohenlohe, *Carte Theiner* 4/905 (10 October 1857); the imperial gift in Goldinger, *Archivalische Zeitschrift*, XLVII (1951), 24 n. 8; H. Jedin brought out the remarkable relations between Hohenlohe and Theiner in *Römische Quartalschrift*, LXVI (1971), 171–86. Jedin thought that the diary of Massarelli in question was none of the private diaries but Massarelli's Acta as official secretary, kept in *Concilio*, CXVI; cf. H. Jedin, 'Das Publikationsverbot der Monumenta Tridentina Augustin Theiners im Jahre 1858', *Annuarium Historiae Conciliorum*, III (1971), 91.

10 *Archivio Particolare di Pio Nono*, no. 1373; and for these texts see Jedin, *Annuarium Historiae Conciliorum*, III (1971), 93–8.

11 *Archivio Particolare di Pio Nono*, no. 1380.

12 *Carte Theiner*, 4/905. The commission, before the addition of Gigli and Vercellone on 25 May 1858, consisted of Cardinal Gaude, O.P. (chairman), Tommaso della Tosa, O.P., Professor Filippo Cossa, and the Servite Father Gavino Secchi-Murro. None was a Jesuit. Gigli was the former vicar-general of the Dominicans. That Gigli was liberal-minded was shown in 1868 when he was forced to resign as Maestro del Sacro Palazio (an office he held from 1859) because one of his colleagues gave an imprimatur to too liberal a book; cf. Jedin, *Annuarium Historiae Conciliorum*, III (1971), 91.

13 Cf. *Archivio Particolare di Pio Nono*, no, 1679; Theiner, Lettera relativa ad alcuni Giornali Protestanti Tedeschi stampati in S. Luigi nell'America.

14 V. Conzemius, *Ignaz von Döllinger: Briefwechsel mit Lord Acton*, I (Munich 1963–71), 462. For Acton's early view of Theiner, as one who edited indispensable and otherwise unobtainable documents, but edited them badly, see the article 'Father Theiner's Publications' in *The Rambler*, x (London 1858), 265ff.

15 Conzemius, *Briefwechsel*, I, 406.

16 McElrath, *Lord Acton: the Decisive Decade*, 133.

17 Acton to Döllinger, Rome, Christmas 1866; Conzemius, *Briefwechsel*, I, 456.

18 McElrath, *Lord Acton: the Decisive Decade*, 135. Acton still possessed the draft preface in 1895.

19 *Saturday Review*, 1874, 304. According to a letter from Acton to Döllinger (Aldenham, 19 September 1874, Conzemius, *Briefwechsel*, III, 126) the material for the article was taken from a letter from Acton. This must be understood largely, for the authorship is unmistakable from style, content, information, and even quotations.

20 Theiner to Acton, 31 October 1865, Acton Papers, Box 10; I am grateful to Mr R. V. Kerr of Cambridge University Library for decipherment of Theiner's difficult script.

21 Johannes Janssen to Frau von Sydow, 3–7 April 1864; Ludwig
   von Pastor (ed.), *Johannes Janssen's Briefe*, I
   (Freiburg-im-Breisgau 1920), 296.
22 Reprinted in *The History of Freedom and other Essays*, ed. J. N.
   Figgis & R. V. Laurence (London 1907), 101ff.
23 *History of Freedom*, 102. For a modern treatment, see H.
   Butterfield, *Man on his Past* (London 1955); C. H. V.
   Sutherland, *The Massacre of St Bartholomew and the European
   Conflict, 1559–1572* (London 1973); and P. Hurtubise,
   'Comment Rome apprit la nouvelle du massacre...',
   Archivium Historiae Pontificiae, x (1972), 187–209.
24 Mackintosh, *History of England*, III, 354; Theiner, *Annales
   ecclesiastici 1572–1585*, I (3 vols., Rome 1856), 328.
25 Theiner thought that Chateaubriand took the copies of Salviati
   when he was a diplomat in Rome. Acton thought that he took
   them while the papal archives were in Paris. But Viennot told
   Acton (17 July 1869, Acton Papers, Box 10) that Chateaubriand
   made his copy when in Rome during 1818.
26 Cambridge University Library, Add. Mss., 4843, 4845.
27 McElrath, *Lord Acton: The Decisive Decade*, 135.
28 *History of Freedom*, 102.
29 Conzemius, *Briefwechsel*, III, 284; 16 June 1882. The list is
   Theiner, Newman, Falloux, Hefele.
30 McElrath, *Lord Acton: the Decisive Decade*, 133–4.
31 *Vetera Monumenta* (1863), documents on the history of the
   Southern Slav peoples. Strossmayer got to know Theiner when
   he visited Rome during 1860, cf. H. Jedin, 'Augustin Theiner',
   Archiv für schlesische Kirchengeschichte, XXXI, 135–86, also
   printed separately (Hildesheim 1973); indispensable for
   Theiner's relations to Germany. Strossmayer paid the expense
   of printing the 1863 volume.
32 Father Piccirillo, who edited *Civiltà Cattolica*: cf. Acton to
   Döllinger, 5 June 1870, Conzemius, *Briefwechsel*, II, 410. For the
   atmosphere that Theiner was out of step at the end of the
   eighteen-sixties, see the information laid against his book on
   the Two Concordats. The book praised Napoleon I to excess
   for what he had done for the Church. The Pope was sent two
   critical memoranda on the book and the spirit in which it was
   written. The memoranda in effect reported that Theiner was a
   well-intentioned eccentric. Cf. the memoranda in *Archivio
   Particolare di Pio Nono*, no. 2108. This charge of eccentricity fits
   a phrase written by Alfred von Reumont in a passage where
   he gave high praise to Theiner's services to history – that there
   was something *cross-eyed* about Theiner's vision. Cf. Reumont,
   Aus König Friedrich Wilhelms IV gesunden und kranken Tagen
   (Leipzig 1885), 543.

33 *Entzückt*: Conzemius, *Briefwechsel*, II, 58. For Acton's reputation
   in Rome, early that year, as the probable author of Quirinus,
   see F. Gregorovius, *Römische Tagebücher*, 2nd edn (Stuttgart
   1893), *ap.* 18 February and 10 March 1870.

34 Gisiger, *Theiner*, 53.

35 Sickel, preface to J. Šusta, *Die Römische Curie und das Concil
   von Trient unter Pius IV*, IV (4 vols., Vienna 1904–14).

36 Probably Forbes of Brechin was meant. Among the Theiner
   papers are only two letters from Forbes to Theiner, *Carte
   Theiner*, 1/1102–4. Forbes and Acton once dined with Theiner
   in the Tower of the Winds.

37 Quirinus, *Letters from Rome*, Eng. trans. (London 1870), 194.

38 *Saturday Review*, 1874, 304.

39 Gisiger, *Theiner*, 56–61. Cf. Gregorovius, *Tagebücher*, 315.
   Theiner's sense that the Jesuits particularly suspected him
   because of what he allowed Acton to see appears in Theiner's
   letter to Acton of 13 December 1865, Acton Papers, Box 10.

40 McElrath, *Lord Acton: the Decisive Decade*, 93. For Acton's
   request to come and take his leave, Acton to Theiner, 10 June
   1870, *Carte Theiner*, 1/1.

41 Gisiger, *Theiner*, 53. See also an unpublished letter from
   Friedrich to Acton, Kufstein, 21 August 1890, Acton Papers,
   Box 10: When I brought with me from Rome the modus
   procedendi of Trent in the Theiner printing, Döllinger
   thought it important for the Vatican Council and caused me to
   print the same in my Documents of the Vatican Council – from
   a Munich manuscript which I tracked down, in order to spare
   Theiner. This had only an *ad hoc* aim.

42 *Documenta ad illustranda Concilium Vaticanum*, I (Nördlingen,
   1871), 265: Jedin, *Erforschung*, 186. Hefele saw the Tridentine
   Acts in the spring of 1869 and did not need Theiner's help,
   Quirinus, *Letters*, Eng. trans., 655–6.

43 Ludwig von Pastor, *Tagebücher, Briefe, Erinnerungen*, ed. W.
   Wühr (Heidelberg 1950), 31 August 1874; 14 November 1876.

44 Theiner to Friedrich, 29 November 1872: *Kölnische Zeitung* in
   Gisiger, *Theiner*, 94. For an almost similar description of
   scholars coming to him to complain that they could not get
   what they wanted from those in charge of the archives, see
   Theiner to Acton, Foro d'Ischia, 25 September 1873, Acton
   Papers, Box 23. The 'little clergyman' was Debellini, of whose
   inaccuracy Marino Marini complained to Theiner shortly
   before his death, 27 October 1854, *Carte Theiner*, 3.

45 Cf. *Carte Theiner*, 4/157.

46 *Carte Theiner*, 1/804.

47 Theiner to Friedrich, 30 August 1870, Foro d'Ischia: printed in
   Kölnische Zeitung and by Gisiger, *Theiner*, 79–80. For Cardoni's

friendship with Theiner, see Theiner to Acton, 10 June 1870,
Acton Papers, Box 23. The same letter contains Theiner's view
of Cristofori. For Cardoni's appointment, VSA, Secretary of
State, Rubricella 1870, no. 59194; June 1870.

48 Gisiger, *Theiner*, 67, 70.
49 *Saturday Review*, 1874, 304. Theiner's friendship with members
of the conquering Italian administration in Rome helped the
Oratory in Vallicella to retain part of its old premises when so
much other ecclesiastical property was nationalized. His old
friend and superior Carlo Rossi wrote him letters of heartfelt
gratitude. The Oratory never regarded him as other than a
loyal son. See *Carte Theiner*, 4/816, 820: Carlo Rossi to Theiner,
14 April 1871 and 10 March 1873; Theiner to the Italian
minister Gadda, *Carte Theiner*, 2/24 and ff.; also in Oratory
papers (Vallicella), Theiner III. The help which Theiner gave
Domenico Berti over the Galileo papers was useful in this
connection: see Theiner, Oratory Papers (Vallicella),
III, Theiner's letter of 1 April 1871.
50 Long letter in German, Herrnsheim, 6 October 1873, *Carte
Theiner*, 1/3.
51 Strossmayer to Theiner, 20 January 1870, Oratory Papers
(Vallicella); and Jedin, *Theiner*, 170.
52 *Saturday Review*, 1874, 304.
53 Pastor's *Tagebücher*, 99; 15 March 1877. Theiner's attack on
Ranke in the preface to *Schweden und seine Stellung...*(1838);
partially compensated by praise of Ranke in the study of the
massacre of St Bartholomew in the three volumes on Pope
Gregory XIII. Some of the language in the preface to *Schweden*
helps to show why Acton never forgot that this was the son of
a Breslau cobbler. 'Ranke has had the audacity and arrogance
to tell the public, like some quack advertising his wares, of a
so-called History of the Popes', etc. etc.
54 Quirinus, *Letters*, Eng. trans., Letter no. 46, p. 536; Letter no.
57, p. 655.
55 Cf. Jedin, *Theiner*, 172; from Geslin in *Le Clocher*, VII (1874–5),
214; for still earlier evidence, *Osservatore Romano*, 11 August
1874, n. 181; Angelo Mercati, 'Il sommario del processo di
Giordano Bruno', *Studi e testi*, CI (1942), preface.

CHAPTER 5

1 Sickel, *Römische Erinnerungen*, 184. *Osservatore Romano* of 21
December 1870 strongly affirmed the Vatican to be the sole
property of the Pope; and the Italian government contented
itself with a platonic statement that the Vatican collections are
part of the Italian literary and artistic heritage; Albert

Battandier, *Le Cardinal J. B. Pitra, évêque de Porto* (Paris 1893), 774.

2 Best account of the history of the text of *Liber Diurnus* in the preface to the edition by Hans Foerster, *Liber Diurnus Romanorum Pontificum* (Berne 1958).

3 Daremberg's recommendation of Rozière to Theiner, dated 26 March 1862, in *Carte Theiner*, 1/762; he asked to see (1) the Croce manuscript, (2) Holste's suppressed edition, (3) Holste's notes, of which a copy was known to have existed in the library of Cardinal Zelada, and of which Gaetano Marini made a copy. Sickel was the first to take the *Liber Diurnus* as a historical document out of the realm of controversy, in his edition of 1889. He used only the Vatican manuscript because that of Claremont had vanished. When the Jesuits were suppressed, the Claremont manuscript was acquired by the Dutchman Gerhard Meerman, afterwards Mayor of Rotterdam. Meerman's son sold his father's manuscripts to Sir Thomas Phillipps but not the *Liber Diurnus*. It was discovered in an antique shop in 1937 and given to the Benedictine Abbey of Egmond-Binnen in Holland. Meanwhile, shortly after Sickel's edition of the Vatican manuscript, the prefect of the Ambrosian Library in Milan gave notice that he had a manuscript. Today the text rests on the three manuscripts, Vatican, Claremont, Ambrosian.

4 Sickel was staying there working at the Arco manuscripts of Trent and reports it in *Römische Erinnerungen*, 169ff.

5 Alfred von Arneth, *Aus meinem Leben*, II (Vienna 1892), 325–6. Italy demanded the archives back. A conference met in Milan and reached a compromise on what papers should return.

6 Sickel, *Römische Erinnerungen*, 135–6, 169–70; an episode considered by H. Butterfield, *Man on his Past*, and *Historical Journal*, XV (1972), 825–6. *Römische Erinnerungen* was edited by Santifaller with a second part of valuable documents.

7 Acton to Marie, 17–20 October 1870, Acton Papers, Box 19. Further evidence in Conzemius, *Briefwechsel*, II, 449ff.; E. S. Purcell, *Life of Cardinal Manning*, 2nd edn, II (London 1896), 466; Acton to Sickel, Munich, 12 November 1870, printed by Santifaller, 251–2 (*ap.* Sickel's *Römische Erinnerungen*).

8 Quirinus, *Letters*, Eng. trans., Letter 59, p. 693. Short memoir of Father Piccirillo, *Civiltà Cattolica*, series 13, XI, (1888), 624. On 20 June 1870 the Bavarian ambassador to the Vatican, Tauffkirchen, reported to his government that Roman society is surprised that the Pope allows Piccirillo to work unsupervised in the archives, and that Piccirillo makes daily use of the permission; from Bavarian state archives, cited E. Kessler, *Johann Friedrich (1836–1917)* (*Miscellanea Bavarica*

Monacensia, LV), Munich 1975, 205. At the time of the Vatican Council Father Piccirillo had frequent access to Pope Pius IX, not less than once a fortnight; and Archbishop Manning was once kept waiting so that Piccirillo could see the Pope. See J. Beumer, 'Ein neu veröffentlichtes Tagebuch zum ersten Vatikanum', *Annuarium Historiae Conciliorum*, VI (1974), 406.

9 Quirinus, *Letters*, Eng. trans., Letter 59, p. 693.

10 Kaltenbrunner to Sickel, Rome, 5 February 1879; Santifaller (*ap.* Sickel, *Römische Erinnerungen*), 334–5.

11 £100 per annum: Obituary of Stevenson in *Jesuit Letters and Notices*, XXIII (1895–6), 117ff.

12 Acton to Master of the Rolls, 15 September 1866; Master of the Rolls to Keeper of Records (T. Duffus Hardy), 20 September; Hardy to Master of the Rolls, 25 September; Master of the Rolls to Acton, 26 September; Acton to Master of the Rolls, 15 October; Master of the Rolls to Hardy, 19 October 1866; Public Record Office 1/31.

13 Master of the Rolls to Treasury, 13 November 1869; Treasury agreement, 30 November; Master of the Rolls to Acton, 3 December; Acton to Master of the Rolls, 21 December 1869; Master of the Rolls to Acton, 13 January 1870; PRO 1/34–35.

14 Hardy to Stevenson, 1 February 1872, PRO 1/37; Stevenson to Hardy, 2 February; further letters of 23, 24, 25, 26 February; acceptance, 27 February 1872.

15 Acton to Richard Simpson, in *The Correspondence of Lord Acton and Richard Simpson*, ed. J. L. Altholz, J. C. Holland & D. McElrath, III (Cambridge 1975), 303.

16 Hardy to Foreign Office, 24 July 1872; Hammond to Hardy, 30 July 1872; PRO 1/37.

17 Copy of printed instructions, PRO 1/37; Vatican copy, Secretary of State, 1872/47/65; Propaganda copy, *Scritture Riferite nei Congressi*, Anglia 19 (1871–4), no. 430.

18 Stevenson's draft of a narrative of his proceedings, Farm Street archives.

19 Debellini to Antonelli, 6 September 1872, VSA, Secretary of State 1872/47/67.

20 Stevenson to Hardy, 30 September 1872; 10 October 1872; PRO 1/37/444 and 465. Stevenson's draft narrative, Farm Street.

21 Hardy to Stevenson, 2 December 1873, PRO 1/38.

22 Stevenson to John Morris, 10 January 1874, Farm Street.

23 Stevenson to John Morris, 25 November 1873, Farm Street.

24 Stevenson to John Morris, Rome, 15 February 1874, Farm Street.

25 Stevenson to Hardy, 21 November 1874, PRO 1/39.

26 Manning to Master of the Rolls, 27 April 1875; PRO 1/40.

27 Stevenson to John Morris, 26 December 1874, Farm Street; the bitter cold gave him pleurisy and he could say no mass on Christmas day.

28 Stevenson to Estcourt, 26 February 1876, Farm Street.

29 Purcell, *Life of Manning*, II, 543. For Sickel's unsuccessful attempt to get access to the archives in 1876, although he had the backing of Cardinals Pitra and Hohenlohe (the latter, though he perhaps did not know it, not an advantage to him), see *Römische Erinnerungen*, 33–4. Not until after March 1876 did Stevenson gain the freedom to range beyond the reign of Henry VIII; cf. Altholz, *Acton–Simpson Correspondence*, III, 336.

30 Stevenson to John Morris, 10 November 1876, Farm Street.

31 Stevenson to John Morris, 8 August 1876, Farm Street.

32 Letter to Cardinal Franchi, Archives of Propaganda, *Scritture Riferite*. Anglia, xx (1875–7), no. 1204; Stonor's memorandum, no. 1206, covering letter of 10 January 1877, no. 1207; Secretary of State's permission, Cardinal Simeoni to Cardinal Franchi, 24 February 1877, no. 1225.

33 Stevenson to Estcourt, 21 November 1876, Farm Street: cf. Bliss to Hardy, 18 January 1877, PRO 1/42.

34 Bliss to Hardy, 15 January 1877, PRO 1/42/38. The letters of Cardinals Cullen and Manning recommending Bliss are in Secretary of State, 1877/47/40 and 44.

35 *L'Histoire et l'oeuvre de l'Ecole française de Rome* (Paris 1931), 256; Auguste Geffroy, *L'Ecole française de Rome, ses origines...* (1884); Catalogue of the Exhibition of *L'Ecole française de Rome 1875–1975* (1975); R. Cagnat, 'Notices sur la vie et les travaux de M. Elie Berger', *Comptes rendus de l'Académie des Inscriptions* (1926), 262ff; E. Berger, in *Bibliothèque de l'Ecole des Chartes*, LXIV, 444.

36 The archivist of the King of Saxony, Otto Posse, got leave in 1877, to see Saxon documents to 1486, always 'under the eye of an archivist' and 'according to the rules in force'. Cf. Secretary of State, 1876/67/3; 1877/47/3 and 7 and 9; Posse, *Analecta Vaticana*, 1878.

37 Fierce comments on Hergenröther's hat in F. X. Kraus, *Tagebücher* (Cologne 1957), 398.

38 Count Paar to Andrássy, 13 June 1879: Santifaller, *ap.* Sickel, *Römische Erinnerungen*, 466–7. That summer a cleric visiting Austria told Sickel, who failed to get access in 1876, to try again; and Sickel believed him a messenger sent by Hergenröther; Sickel, *Römische Erinnerungen*, 36.

39 So A. Gottlob, 'Das Vaticanische Archiv', *Historisches Jahrbuch*, VI (1885), 279.

40 For Balan, see *Dizionario biografico degli Italiani, s.v.* (1963); *Enciclopedia cattolica*, (Citta del Vaticano 1949–54); A. Gambasin,

'Pietro Balan Storiografo apologista del papato', *Archivum Historiae Pontificiae*, IV (1966), 349–54.

41 Gindely of Prag to Conrad von Eybesfeld, 2 June 1882, from archives of the Austrian Ministry of Education, in Hans Kramer, *Das Österreichische Historische Institut in Rom, 1881–1931* (Rome 1932), 6. Sickel remained anxious throughout that decade. He took the trouble to get both Hergenröther and Balan made Commanders of the imperial order of Francis-Joseph; later he helped to persuade Innsbruck University to give an honorary degree to Denifle.

42 The next oldest national institute after the Ecole française. Sickel began work in the archives in April 1881, one of the first. They wanted to imitate the French by having rooms with the Austrian embassy, that is, in the Palazzo Venezia, but the embassy would not agree.

43 *Römische Erinnerungen*, 57–8. The edition, with a valuable preface, was published at Innsbruck in 1883 as *Das Privilegium Otto I für die Römische Kirche vom Jahre 962*. In addition to Hergenröther's memorandum, Camillo Rè wrote a memorandum in the same sense. It is clear that this obscure but interesting lawyer had private influence among the Pope's entourage. Sickel's wife was the daughter of a well-known Austrian architect; a shy woman, delicate in health.

44 Cambridge University Library, Add. Mss. 4931, 206; 5015, 54; Butterfield, *Man on His Past*, 84.

45 Add. Ms. 4929, 46; Butterfield, *Man on His Past*, 77.

46 Reported (e.g.) *The Times*, 4 April 1882. After the Vespers of 1282 the barons and city representatives held their meeting at the church of the Martorana.

47 Leo XIII, *Acta*, III, 264–5; even earlier, when the Sicilian bishops protested to him against part of the celebration of the Sicilian Vespers, he wrote a letter (22 April 1882) on all the popes had done for Sicily; Tserclaes, *Leo XIII*, I, 361–2. His sub-archivist Monsignor Pietro Balan wrote a controversial study of Sicily and the popes with reference to Garibaldi's letter, Crispi, Perez, and the Pope's letter: cf. P. Balan, *I Papi e il Vespro Siciliano*, with unpublished documents (Rome 1882). The idea of the Popes as defenders of Italy was not new in Leo. It goes back to de Maistre's *Du Pape*, Rosmini's *Panegirico di Pio VII*, Manzoni's *Discorso...della Storia Longobardica*, etc.: cf. also Candeloro, *Storia d'Italia*, II, 352.

48 Giovanni Spadolini, *L'Opposizione cattolica da Porta Pia al '98* (Florence 1954), 186.

49 Heidler to Foreign Secretary Kálnoky, Rome, 31 August 1883; Santifaller, *ap*. Sickel, *Römische Erinnerungen*, 469–70.

50 Tserclaes, *Leo XIII*, II, 371; Pastor described the scene in *Tagebücher*, 24 February 1884.

51 Battandier, *Pitra*, 643ff. Cardinal de Luca's health was broken and he soon died. After Pitra's resignation, the three commissioners were Hergenröther, Parocchi, Bartolini: cf. *Civiltà Cattolica*, series 12, VII (1884), 599.

52 Purcell, *Life of Manning*, 2nd edn, II, 581. For Marcellino da Civezza's endeavours see *Il Romano pontificato nella storia d'Italia* (Florence 1886), 2nd edn, 1889; and for the whole story of this task, see Riccardo Pratesi, 'Il P. Marcellino da Civezza, O.F.M.: vita e scritti', *Archivum Franciscanum Historicum*, XLIII (1950), 243–334.

53 Elie Berger the French Protestant was already far advanced on the register of Innocent IV; Hergenröther on that of Leo X. They had an argument on the commission whether they should publish the register as in the manuscript (Pitra, Berger) or by chronological arrangement (Hergenröther). The commission accepted the former, as easier, less time-consuming and less liable to error; leaving Hergenröther to go his own way, Battandier, *Pitra*, 651–2. For the printing machines cf. *Civiltà Cattolica*, series 12, VII (1884), 599.

54 Sickel, *Römische Erinnerungen*, 98.

55 Heidler to Foreign Minister Kálnoky, Rome, 28 September 1883, in Santifaller, *ap.* Sickel, *Römische Erinnerungen*, Santifaller, 477; Sickel, *Römische Erinnerungen*, 63. Balan's letter of 28 October 1883 was published in *La voce della verità*, 4–5 November, and in *Civiltà Cattolica*, series 12, IV (1883), 496ff. Balan's receipt, and a contract, for the faintly odd money transactions with the Austrians, in Goldinger, *Archivalische Zeitschrift*, XLVII (1951), 47–8.

56 The first plan was to persuade Johannes Janssen from Frankfurt to come. The probable appointment was even announced in the newspapers; cf. Santifaller, *ap.* Sickel, *Römische Erinnerungen*, 384; and *Tablet* (1883), 604. On 1 May 1884 the Pope issued a new *motuproprio* on the archives (for this and the change of plan over publishing it, see Gottlob, *Historisches Jahrbuch*, VI (1885), 279–80; Sickel, *Römische Erinnerungen*, 66–7; Goldinger, *Archivalische Zeitschrift*, XLVII (1951), 36). Together with Denifle came Monsignor Delicati, 1883–95.

57 The Congress was of April 1898; the attack by Joseph Hansen, who worked at the German Institute in Rome and from 1891 was director of the city archive at Cologne: cf. Sickel's report to Vienna, 19 June 1898, in Santifaller, *ap.* Sickel, *Römische Erinnerungen*, 237ff. When in 1888 Schottmüller began work for

the Prussian Historical Institute he was not given access to catalogues and had to depend on Denifle, Walter Friedensburg, *Abhandlungen der königlich Preussischen Akademie der Wissenschaften*, I (1903), 29–30 but not for long, *ibid.*, 48–9.

58 Kraus, *Tagebücher*, 551. Kraus took the chance of a private audience to complain to Pope Leo (6 April 1889).

59 Johannes Haller, *Lebenserinnerungen*, ed. R. Wittram (Stuttgart 1960), 122.

CHAPTER 6

1 *Kirchengeschichte*, II, 129–33, 4th edn (1904), II, 982–3. For Massimo d'Azeglio's belief (writing in 1863) that as a boy he was not allowed to learn medieval history lest he learn of (among others) Alexander VI, see *I mei Ricordi*, Eng. trans. (1966), 53.

2 M. Ollivier, Paris 1870 (one volume only published); F. Kayler, Regensburg 1878; Andrea Leonetti, 3 vols., Bologna 1880.

3 The 'latest historian' was Gregorovius.

4 Walburga Lady Paget, *Scenes and Memories* (London 1912), 208.

5 Flir, *Briefe aus Rom*, 114, ein gefangenes Teufelchen. Achille Gennarelli published an edition, inadequate, of the diary at Florence, 1854; excerpts were published by Leibniz (Hanover 1697).

6 Kurd von Schlözer, *Römische Briefe 1864–1869*, 12th edn, ed. Karl von Schlözer (Berlin 1922), 203ff. (31 March 1865).

7 H. de l'Epinois, in *Revue des questions historiques*, XXIX (1881), 357ff., the letter of Pope Pius II dated 14 June 1460; which Rinaldi put into his continuation of Baronius.

8 Vilnios Fraknói, 1843–1924; 1865 professor of the seminary at Gran, and various titles afterwards including a titular bishopric 1892 and a titular abbey 1900; but he spent most of his later years in Rome as the inspector of the Hungarian Historical Institute which he founded; Santifaller, *ap.* Sickel, *Römische Erinnerungen*, 66n.

9 Pastor used the registers of Alexander VI, and Sickel wondered whether he got leave before November 1885. But Pastor says (preface to the 1st edn of III, compare the preface to the English translation to v) that through Cardinal Hergenröther he got the Pope's leave in spring 1888, that is, two and a half years after the Fraknói–Sickel raid; and Pastor says that until he saw them, no one else had been allowed to see them for three hundred years. But despite the dust in the Lateran Archive, Sickel and Fraknói could see the volumes laid aside for the use of Hergenröther. They also knew that, a few months before, the state archivist of Saxony, Posse, had got

into the Lateran Archive, though only for a couple of hours; Santifaller, *ap.* Sickel, *Römische Erinnerungen*, 212.

10 Sickel learnt this from Tosti in November 1885, who himself learnt it from Leo's lips; Santifaller, *ap.* Sickel, *Römische Erinnerungen*, 212.

11 Sickel, *Römische Erinnerungen*, 84, 213.

12 P. M. Baumgarten, *Römische und andere Erinnerungen* (Düsseldorf 1927), 196–7.

13 Pastor, *Tagebücher*, 28 February 1875. The atmosphere of this school of Catholic history in the age of the Kulturkampf is perceptively analysed by H. Srbik, *Geist und Geschichte*, II, *vom deutschen Humanismus bis zur Gegenwart* (Salzburg 1950–1), 6off.

14 S. Skalweit, *Lexikon für Theologie und Kirche, s.v.* Klopp.

15 Pastor, *Tagebücher*, 114–15, 20 September 1878; cf. 93 and 97, 14 November 1876 and 13 February 1877.

16 *Janssen's Briefe*, II, 82.

17 Pastor, *Tagebücher*, 169–70.

18 *Göttingische gelehrte Anzeige*, nr. 12 June 1887, 449–93. For the 'Prussian' view see *Historische Zeitschrift*, LVII (1887), 272ff. – has learning and accuracy, impossible not to see an apologetic tendency, some paragraphs belong more to a compendium of dogmatics than a history, etc. The Pope's brief was dated 20 January 1887.

19 *Civiltà Cattolica*, series 16, v (1896), 591ff., 710ff. *English Historical Review* (Richard Garnett), July 1897, 559. Pastor complained warmly in his diary that the *Historische Zeitschrift* was publicly contemptuous by refusing even to notice the book; but the review when it came at last (by Kawerau, *Historische Zeitschrift*, LXXX (1898), 299ff.) was the most favourable which that weighty journal had yet given to Pastor. For other examples of praise from widely different viewpoints, see (e.g.) *Archivio storico italiano*, XVII (1896), 423ff. *Jahresberichte der Geschichtswissenschaft*, XIX (1896), iii, 51; *Dublin Review*, CXVIII (1896), 309 (T. B. Scannell). For the final surrender of *Historische Zeitschrift*, see XC (1906), 467ff.; CV (1910), 361ff. At the popular level the reputation stayed longer. In 1899 the Viennese journal *Die Fackel* was glad that Pastor never became professor of history at Vienna for he would only have preached pious legends. Cf. Georg Janković, 'Krisenjahre des Österreichischen Historischen Instituts in Rom (1914–24)', *Römische Historische Mitteilungen* (1971), 187n.

20 By Steinmann in *Allgemeine Zeitung*, 20 December 1899; cf. Pastor, *Tagebücher, ad diem*: 'this noble Protestant'.

21 Pastor, *Tagebücher*, 25 June 1897.

22 Pastor, *Tagebücher*, 25 November 1906; 28 December 1920; cf. 19 December 1921; 12 October 1897; 31 January 1901. For

Cardinal Gaetano de Lai's importance in the Vatican, see F. Engel-Jánosi, *Österreich und der Vatikan*, II (Graz 1958), 137, 178; for Cardinal Tommaso Pio Boggiani's attitude (Cardinal 1916–42) see A. Pelzer, 'L'historien Louis von Pastor d'après ses journaux, sa correspondance et ses souvenirs', *Revue d'histoire ecclésiastique*, XLVI (1951), 195.

23 Haller, *Lebenserinnerungen*, 121; commented by L. Santifaller, 'Bemerkungen zu den "Lebenserinnerungen" von Johannes Haller', *Römische Historische Mitteilungen*, V (1961–2), 170.

24 Monsignor Tosti was vice-archivist till 1891. But he was used in private negotiations with the Italian government, and became almost titular at the archives even before he resigned. Cf. Kraus, *Tagebücher*, 667–8. He was forced out because he published *La Conciliazione* (1887), which wanted reconciliation with the Italian government and was contrary to the policy of the Curia.

25 So Ehrle, an unimpeachable source, told Pastor, *Tagebücher*, 20 July 1903.

26 Sickel, *Römische Erinnerungen*, 142.

27 Fraknói to Sickel, 11 August 1894; printed (L. Santifaller) in *Römische Historische Mitteilungen*, VI–VII (1963–4), 236–7; cf. Santifaller's review of Johannes Haller's *Lebenserinnerungen*, *ibid.* (1961–2), 170–2; Engel-Jánosi, *Österreich und der Vatikan*, I, 262.

28 *Civiltà Cattolica*, series 17, IX (1900), 356–7.

29 Fraknói to Sickel, 29 May 1884, printed by L. Santifaller, in *Römische Historische Mitteilungen*, VII (1963–4), 215. For Denifle, A. Walz in *Dictionnaire d'histoire et de géographie ecclésiastiques*; Grabmann, Bertold Waldstein-Wartemberg; Sickel, *Römische Erinnerungen*, 252ff. *et al.*; H. Grauert, *Historisches Jahrbuch*, XXVI (1905), 959–1018, also published separately with revisions; I. P. Kirsch, *Revue d'histoire ecclésiastique*, VI (1905), 665–76; Haller, *Lebenserinnerungen*, 179–81.

30 Document dated 12 December 1580 (Cardinal of Como to nuncio Segna), first printed by A. O. Meyer, *England und die Katholische Kirche in England unter Elisabeth*, I (1911), Appendix 18B, p. 428. For this story about Denifle, P. M. Baumgarten, *Römische und andere Erinnerungen*, 106ff.; L. Santifaller, in *Römische Historische Mitteilungen*, V (1961–2), 169.

31 Sickel, *Römische Erinnerungen*, 65, 101.

32 Angelo Mercati, *Studi e testi*, CI (1942), 21.

33 F. Meinecke, 'Ausgewählte Briefwechsel', in *Werke* VI (Munich 1962), 87; Santifaller, in *Römische Historische Mitteilungen*, V (1961–2), 169, n. 13. D. Mack Smith, *Victor Emanuel, Cavour and the Risorgimento* (London 1971), viii–ix.

34 *Concilii Tridentini Diariorum Pars Prima*, ed. S. Merkle (Freiburg-im-Breisgau 1901), ix–xi.
35 Haller, *Lebenserinnerungen*, 184–6; Pastor, *Tagebücher*, 5 May 1902.
36 Cf. S. Steinberg, *Die Geschichtswissenschaft der Gegenwart in Selbstdarstellungen*, II (Leipzig 1926), 186.
37 Pastor, *Tagebücher*, 17 October 1903; cf. Steinberg, II, 186.
38 Fraknói to Sickel, Rome, 9 January 1904; printed by L. Santifaller, in *Römische Historische Mitteilungen*, VI–VII (1963–4), 293.
39 From 1919 the Cardinal-librarian and Cardinal-archivist were the same person: Gasquet 1919–29, Ehrle 1929–34, Giovanni Mercati 1936–57, Tisserant 1957–71, Samorè 1974– .
40 Pastor, *History of the Popes*, Eng. trans., XXV, 99 n. 4.
41 Cf. Pastor, *Geschichte*, German edn, III, 2, 5–7 edd. (1924), Anhang 56.

CHAPTER 7

1 Lietzmann's obituary of Ehrle in *Deutsche Allgemeine Zeitung*, 31 March 1934; quoted K. Christ, *Zentralblatt für Bibliothekswesen*, LII (1935), 23.
2 Pastor, *Tagebücher*, 22 March 1902; informant Montel; cf. 29 December 1902.
3 Pastor, *Tagebücher*, 5 January 1888; 24 February 1928.
4 Cambridge University Library, Add. Mss. 4929, 121; 4931, 52; 4931, 206.
5 Pastor, *Tagebücher*, 20 May 1925.

Select Bibliography

Acton, Lord: the Decisive Decade, 1864–74, essays and documents, ed. D. McElrath et al., Louvain 1970.

Acton, Lord. See also Conzemius.

Battandier, Albert. Le Cardinal J. B. Pitra, évêque de Porto, Paris 1893.

Baumgarten, P. M. 'Die Verhältnisse am vaticanischen geheimen Archiv', Allgemeine Zeitung (1891), Beilage, no. 94, 108, 120, 301 (23 April, 11 and 26 May, 24 December).

Baumgarten, P. M. Römische und andere Erinnerungen, Düsseldorf 1927.

Berlière, U. 'Aux Archives Vaticanes', Revue Bénédictine, XX (1903), 132–73.

Bignami Odier, Jeanne. La Bibliothèque vaticane de Sixte IV à Pie XI, Vatican City 1973 (Studi e testi, 272).

Boyle, L. E. A survey of the Vatican Archives and of its medieval holdings, Pontifical Institute of Medieval Studies, Toronto 1972.

Butterfield, H. Man on his Past, Cambridge 1955.

Conzemius, V. Ignaz von Döllinger: Briefwechsel mit Lord Acton, 3 vols., Munich 1963–71.

Diener, H. Die grossen Registerserien im Vatikanischen Archiv 1378–1523: Hinweise und Hilfsmittel zu ihrer Benutzung und Auswertung, Tübingen 1972.

Dudík, B. Iter Romanum, Vienna 1855.

Fink, K. A. Das Vatikanische Archiv, 2nd edn, Rome 1951.

Flir, Alois. Briefe aus Rom, 2nd edn, ed. L. Rapp, Innsbruck 1864.

Friedensburg, Walter. Das königlich Preussische Historische Institut in Rom in den dreizehn ersten Jahren seines Bestehens, 1888–1901. In Abhandlungen der königlich Preussischen Akademie der Wissenschaften, Phil. Hist. Kl., 1903, no. 1.

Gachard, Louis Prosper. Les archives du Vatican, Brussels 1874.

Gebler, Carl von. Galileo Galilei and the Roman Curia, Eng. trans., London 1879.

Gisiger, Hermann. P. Theiner und die Jesuiten, Mannheim 1875.

Goldinger, W. 'Österreich und die Eröffnung des Vatikanischen Archivs', Archivalische Zeitschrift, XLVII (1951), 23–52.

Grabmann, M. *P. Heinrich Denifle, OP: Eine Würdigung seiner Forschungsarbeit*, Mainz 1905.

Gregorovius, F. *Römische Tagebücher*, 2nd edn, Stuttgart 1893, Eng. trans. 1907.

Haller, Johannes. *Lebenserinnerungen*, ed. R. Wittram, Stuttgart 1960.

Janssen, Johannes. *J. F. Böhmers Leben, Briefe und kleinere Schriften*, 3 vols., Freiburg-im-Breisgau 1868.

Janssen, Johannes, Briefe, ed. Ludwig von Pastor, 2 vols., Freiburg-im-Breisgau 1920.

Jedin, Hubert. *Augustin Theiner*, 1973. Separately printed from *Archiv für schlesische Kirchengeschichte*, XXXI, 135–86.

Jedin, Hubert. 'Briefe Constantin Höflers an Augustin Theiner 1841 bis 1845', *Historisches Jahrbuch*, XCI (1971), 118–27.

Jedin, Hubert. 'Gustav Hohenlohe an Augustin Theiner 1850–70', *Römische Quartalschrift*, LXVI (1971), 171–86.

Jedin, Hubert. 'Kirchenhistorikerbriefe an Augustin Theiner', *Römische Quartalschrift*, LXVI (1971), 187–231.

Jedin, Hubert. *Das Konzil von Trient: ein Überblick über die Erforschung seiner Geschichte*, Rome 1948 (*Storia e letteratura*, XIX).

Jedin, Hubert. 'Das Publikationsverbot der Monumenta Tridentina Augustin Theiners im Jahre 1858', *Annuarium Historiae Conciliorum*, III, Paderborn 1971, 89–97.

Kramer, H. *Das Österreichische Historische Institut in Rom 1881–1931*, Rome 1932.

Kraus, F. X. *Tagebücher*, Cologne 1957.

Leclercq, H. 'Marini, Gaetano', in *Dictionnaire d'archéologie chrétienne et de liturgie*.

L'Histoire et l'œuvre de l'Ecole française de Rome, Paris 1931.

Lösch, Stephan, *Prof. Dr Adam Gengler*, Würzburg 1963, 197–215 (on Theiner).

Macfarlane, L. 'The Vatican Archives: with special reference to sources for British medieval history', *Archives*, IV (1959), no. 21, 29–44; no. 22, 84–101.

Marini, Marino. *Memorie storiche dell'occupazione e restituzione degli Archivii della Santa Sede*; printed in *Regestum Clementis V*, Rome 1885, prolegomena.

Mauri, Achille. 'Agostino Theiner', *Archivio storico italiano*, XXI (1875), 350–91.

Mélanges Eugène Tisserant, IV–V, Vatican 1964 (*Studi e testi*, 234–5).

Mercati, Angelo. 'Como e quando ritornò a Roma il codice del processo di Galileo', *Atti della Pontificia Accademia delle Scienze Nuove Lincei*, LXXX (1926), 58–63.

Mercati, Angelo. *Il sommario del processo di Giordano Bruno*, Rome 1942 (*Studi e testi*, 101).

Pastor, Ludwig von. *Tagebücher, Briefe, Erinnerungen*, ed. W. Wühr, Heidelberg 1950.

Pastor, Ludwig von. See also Janssen, Johannes and Steinberg, S.

Pertz, G. H. *Autobiography and letters*, ed. Leonora Pertz, Eng. trans., London 1894.

Purcell, E. S. *Life of Cardinal Manning*, 2nd edn, 2 vols., London 1896.

Quirinus (pseudonym). *Letters from Rome*, English trans., London 1870.

Ritzler, R. 'Der Verschleppung der päpstlichen Archiv unter Napoleon I', *Römische Historische Mitteilungen*, VI–VII (1962–4).

Santifaller, Leo. 'Bemerkungen zu den "Lebenserinnerungen" von Johannes Haller', *Römische Historische Mitteilungen*, V–VII (1961–4), 164–80.

Santifaller, L. 'Das Österreichische Historische Institut in Rom und die Abteilung für Historische Studien des Österreichisches Kulturinstituts in Rom', *Römische Historische Mitteilungen*, I (1956–7), 5–26.

Santifaller, L. See also Sickel.

Schlözer, Kurd von. *Römische Briefe, 1864–1869*, ed. Karl von Schlözer, 12th edn, Berlin 1922.

Schmidlin, J. *Papstgeschichte der neuesten Zeit*, 4 vols., Munich 1933ff.

Sickel, Theodor von. *Römische Berichte*, 5 parts, 1895–1901 (*Sitzungsberichten d. königl. Akad. der Wiss. in Wien. Phil. Hist. Cl.* 133, ix; 135, x; 141, iv; 143, v; 144, viii).

Sickel, Theodor von. *Römische Erinnerungen: nebst ergänzenden Briefen und Aktenstücken*, ed. L. Santifaller, Vienna 1947 (Veröffentlichungen d. Inst. für Österr. Geschichtsforschung, no. 3).

Sickel, Theodor von. See also Šusta.

Steinberg, Sigfrid. *Die Geschichtswissenschaft der Gegenwart in Selbstdarstellungen*, 2 vols., Leipzig 1926. (II, 168–98 contains a brief autobiography by Pastor.)

Summers, N. and Fletcher, W. A. 'Vatican City', in *Guide to the Diplomatic Archives of Western Europe*, ed. D. H. Thomas & L. M. Case, 1959, 289–307.

Sussidi per la Consultazione dell'Archivio Vaticano, 3 vols, Vatican City 1926–47 (*Studi e testi*, 45, 55, 124).

Šusta, Josef. *Die Römische Curie und das Concil von Trient unter Pius IV*, 4 vols., Vienna 1904–14.

Waldstein-Wartenberg, B. 'Josef Šustas Studienjahre in Rom. Nach dessen Memoiren', *Römische Historische Mitteilungen*, X–XI (1966–9), 127–81.

Walz, A. 'Denifle, H. S.', in *Dictionnaire d'histoire et de géographie ecclésiastiques* (1960).

Index

Acquaviva, Cardinal Trojano, 12
Acton, Cardinal Charles Januarius, 53
Acton, Lord John (1834–1902, Sir John Acton 1837–69, Lord Acton from 1869): aristocrat, 53; pupil of Döllinger, 54, 61, 74; nephew of Cardinal Acton, 53; and Liberal Catholic journals, 53–4; knowledge of languages, 56; visits Rome 1866–7, 53; alliance with Theiner, 54ff., 150; against temporal power, 55; documents of English history, 56, 58; passion for history of Papacy, 36, 53; growing concern over persecution, 56–7; and St Bartholomew's day, 58–61; at Vatican Council, 61ff., 77, 110; part-author of Quirinus, 63; is one of charges against Theiner, 64–5; writes obituary of Theiner, 68–9; his 'raid' on Rome, 72ff.; claims to have helped to open the archives, 76–7; and Stevenson's mission, 77–9; respects Sickel, 98; article on the Borgias, 110; wife, 56, 65, 76, 154; death, 75
on history: history and state secrets 1, 57–8; on the study of archives 98–9, 140–2; Romanes Lecture, never given, 142
Adrian VI (Pope 1522–3), 10
Alciati, Terenzio, Jesuit, 47
Aleander, Cardinal Girolamo, 67
Alexander III (Pope 1159–81), 10
Alexander VI Borgia (Pope 1492–1503), 5, 109ff., 159
Allgemeine Zeitung, 62, 90–1, 163; *see also* Quirinus

Ambrosian Library, 135, 154
Andrássy, Julius, 156
Antonelli, Cardinal Giacomo (1806–76, Pro-Secretary of State from 1848, Secretary of State from 1852): very conservative, 29; prompt in business, 41; urbane, 86; and Marini, 147; and Theiner, 38, 41–2, 49, 65, 67, 79, 149; and Stevenson, 79–85; regarded as illiberal about archives, 87; death, 86
Apollinare, St, in Rome, 28
Aquinas, St Thomas, 101, 130
archives, papal: 5ff.; separated from library, 8–9; incompleteness, 10–11; relation to Secretary of State, 11, 41; cataloguing, 7, 9, 12, 25, 40, 81, 91, 95–6, 107–9, 116, 158–9; French captivity, 14ff.; pressure from governments, 22ff.; pressure from scholars, 39ff.; Theiner's fall, 64ff.; Stevenson inside, 81ff.; complaints about concealment, 90–1; opening to research, 93ff.; first reading room made, 95–6; *motuproprio* of 1884, 158; Balan's fall, 107; Tosti's fall, 161; second reading room made, 127; consultation room (Leonine Library) made, 129–30; heating installed, 129
Augustine of Hippo, St, 34, 101
Avignon, archive at, 5–6, 13
Azeglio, Massimo d', Italian politician, 159

Balan, Pietro: origins, 94; person, 94–6; historian, 94, 106–8, 157; on the German Reformation, 106; on

167

INDEX

Leo XIII (*cont.*)
supports Pastor, 126, 134; gives
Pastor a second brief, 139; gives
leave to Pastor to see documents,
159; and Wenzel, 132; and
Palmieri, 133; and Görres Society,
133; and Inquisition papers, 140;
gives audience to heads of
institutes, 133–4; purchase of
Borghese papers, 11; death, 134
Leonine Library, 129
Letter to the Three Cardinals, 100ff.,
133, 137–8
Liber Diurnus, 14, 72–5, 98, 109, 133,
154
Lietzmann, Hans, 139, 162
Llorente, Juan Antonio, 146
loss of papers, 5, 9–10, 107, 115
Löwenfeld, Samuel, 149
Luther, Martin, 78, 106–7, 131–2

Mabillon, Jean, Benedictine, 3, 56,
73
Macfarlane, Leslie, 144
Mackintosh, Sir James, 59–60
Mai, Cardinal Angelo, 24, 37, 101
Maistre, Joseph de, 157
Manning, Henry Edward (1808–92,
Cardinal 1875–92): Purcell's
biography, 47, 141–2, 154; and
Theiner, 58; and Stevenson, 79,
84–6; and Bliss, 86–7, 156; and
Three Cardinals, 105; sounds
antihistorical, 62, 105; kept
waiting by Pius IX, 155
Manzoni, Alessandro, 157
Marcellino da Civezza, 105, 108
Marcellus II (Pope April–May 1555),
6, 10, 144
Marini, Gaetano, 14, 154
Marini, Marino: nephew of
Gaetano, 16; rescue of archives
from Paris, 16ff.; destroys
Inquisition papers, 18, 139; search
for *Liber Diurnus*, 73; and for
Galileo papers, 19–21; book on
Galileo, 29–30, 42; and Pertz,
22–5; copies of documents for
British Government, 25, 39, 69,
77; and Böhmer, 25–6; doubts
about reliability, 31, 43; and 1848
revolution, 29, 147; needs help
from Theiner, 30–2, 36–7, 42, 48;

proposes Theiner as successor,
37; and Dudík, 147; and
Debellini, 152; death, 38
Massarelli, Angelo, 46, 50–1, 150
Master of the Rolls, *see* Romilly *and*
Jessel
Mendham, Joseph, 48
Mercati, Angelo, 136–7, 146–7, 153
Mercati, Giovanni, 162
Mielli, Martino, 148
Minghetti, Marco, Italian politician,
74
Miollis, General, French
commander in Rome, 14
Möhler, Johann Adam, 110, 148
Montel, Johannes de, 119, 162
Morris, John, Jesuit, 83, 85
Mula, Cardinal Marcantonio da, 6
Munch, Peter Andreas, 41, 148
Müntz, Eugène, 88, 144
Muratori, L. A., 3, 56, 101

Napoleon Bonaparte, 14–15, 19–20,
31, 60, 151
Newman, J. H., 3, 35, 92, 151
Niebuhr, B. G., 22, 87
Nina, Cardinal, 119
nuncios, reports of, 11, 41, 59–60,
131

Oratorians, 14, 32, 35, 38, 48, 63, 70,
92, 149, 153
Osservatore Romano, 153
Oudinot, General, 28

Paar, Count, 156
Paget, Lady Augustus, 110
Palacký, Franz, 146
palaeography, school of, in Vatican,
105–6, 143
Paleotti, Cardinal Gabriele, 48
Pallavicino, Cardinal Pietro, Jesuit,
8, 47–52
Palmieri, Gregorio, 98, 113, 132–3
Parchappe de Vinay, Dr M., 43–4
Parocchi, Cardinal Lucido Maria,
158
Pastor, Ludwig von (1854–1928, till
1916 Ludwig Pastor): early life,
116ff.; pupil of Janssen, 66,
116–17, 124; and *Kulturkampf*, 117,
124, 160; and Ranke, 69, 117–19;
passion for papal history, 36;

171

INDEX

Sarpi, Paolo, 47ff., 69
Sauer, Augustin, 106
Savonarola, Friar, Dominican, 126, 139
Saxony, archivist, see Posse
Saxony, vicar–apostolic in, 12–13, 145
Schott, F., 7, 144
Schottmüller, K., 158–9
Schulte, Aloys, 134
Schulte, Johann Friedrich, 66
Secchi-Murro, Father Gavino, 150
Secretary of State, office of, 11
Segna, Francesco, Cardinal, 129, 134
Sicilian Vespers, 99, 106, 157
Sickel, Theodor (1826–1908, from 1884 von Sickel): meetings with Acton, 74–5; one of first at archives, 157; desire for Palazzo Venezia for Austrian Institute, 157; payment of fees for copies, 96; and *Privilegium Ottonis*, 96–8, 106, 157; and Leo XIII, 97–8, 116, 138; and *Liber Diurnus*, 74–5, 98, 133; Acton's respect for, 98–9; on medieval empire, 106; knowledge of the archives, 109; the 'invasion of the Lateran', 112–16, 159; suspect to some Italians, 115; scholarship of, 115–16; awkwardness with Denifle, 130–3; with Palmieri, 132; staying with Döllinger, 154; reminiscences, 154; gets Austrian awards for archivists, 157; report to Vienna of 1898, 158; and Tosti, 159; wife, 98, 157
Simeoni, Cardinal Giovanni, 87, 89, 156
Sirleto, Girolamo, 6
Sirleto, Guglielmo, 6
Sixtus IV (Pope 1471–84), 5, 9
Sixtus V (Pope 1585–90), 7
Soubise, Palais, archives at, 15ff.
Srbik, H., 160
Steinmann, Ernst, 160
Stevenson, Joseph (1806–95): early career, 77; mission to Rome, 77ff., 136, 156; decision to resign, 84–5; continues at archives, 86–7; unassuming, 89
Stonor, Mgr Edmund, 79–80, 83, 86–7, 90, 156

Storm, Gustav, 148
Strossmayer, Josip, Bishop of Djakovo (Bosnia), 62, 65, 68, 70, 151, 153
Syllabus of Errors (1864), 94

Talbot, George, 54, 141
Tauffkirchen, Count Karl von, 154
Templars, suppression of, 19
Theiner, Anton, 32
Theiner, Augustin (1804–74): early life, 32ff., 56; on celibacy, 32, 34, 147; on canon law, 33, 147; alleged agent, 33, 54; and Lamennais, 34; and Möhler, 148; arrives in Rome, 34, 148; wins Gregory XVI, 34–6; Oratorian, 35, 153; and Newman, 35; on continuing Baronius, 35–6; assists prefect of archives, 36–7, 42; critical of prefect's work, 31; coadjutor to prefect, 32, 152; admired by Mai, 37; his Life of Clement XIV offends Jesuits, 37, 55; prefect of archives, 38, 138, 140; mode of life, 38–9; visitors, 39, 62, 67; as administrator, 39–41; as scholar, 41; on Ranke, 59, 148, 153; on release of Galileo papers, 41ff.; and Berti, 44, 153; and *Liber Diurnus*, 73–4, 154; and Burchard's diary, 111; and documents of Trent, 49ff., 62ff., 68–70, 133; appeals against commission, 51ff., 150; alliance with Acton, 53ff., 62–5, 76–8, 150, 152; and Döllinger, 54–5; and the temporal power, 55; and Jesuits, 55, 152; and the Papacy, 58, 62, 67; and St Bartholomew's day, 58ff.; and the Vatican Council, 62ff., 70; and Strossmayer, 62, 65, 151, 153; 'dismissal', 64–5, 76; last years, 66ff., 80, 152–3; death, 68; reputation, 69–70, 81, 149, 151
Tillemont, Lenain de, 3
Tisserant, Cardinal Eugène, 162
Tosa, Tommaso della, Dominican, 50–1, 150
Tosti, Luigi (1811–97), Benedictine: of Monte Cassino, 107; vice-archivist, 107, 161; looked to by 'Italians' at archives, 115; has

173

INDEX

Tosti (cont.)
  evidence of carelessness under Theiner, 148; on Leo XIII's attitude to Alexander VI, 160; *La Conciliazione*, 161; forced out, 161
Tower of the Winds, the, 38-9, 41, 44, 54, 58, 62, 66-7, 76, 152
Trent, Council of, 1, 8-9, 15, 63ff., 69-70, 106, 133, 152, 154
Tripepi, Luigi, 128

Ullathorne, W. B., Bishop of Birmingham, 79
Umberto I, King of Italy, 102
Urban VI (Pope 1378-89), 148

Valla, Laurentius, 122

Vallicella, Sta Maria Nuova in, 35-6, 38, 143; *see also* Oratorians
Venturi, G., 20
Verallo, Girolamo, 120-1
Vincenzi, 83-4
Visconti-Venosta, Emilio, 67
Voršak, Nikolaus, 70

Waal, Anton de, 119
Wenzel, Pietro: joins staff of archives, 83; freedom with Stevenson, 84-6; and catalogues, 108, 116, 132; help to students, 108-9, 115, 130, 137; and heating, 129; and Palmieri, 133; person, 132
Wühr, W., 120-2, 165

174